SIMPLY 1-2-3 TO SUCCESS

3 Steps to Online Marketing Results!

NIGEL LEAR

Legal Notices

The information presented herein represents the views of the authors as of the date of publication. Because of the rate with which conditions change, the author reserves the right to alter and update his opinion based on the new conditions. This book is for informational purposes only. While every attempt has been made to verify the information provided in this book, neither the authors nor their affiliates/partners assume any responsibility for errors, inaccuracies, or omissions. Any slights of people or organizations are unintentional. You should be aware of any laws which govern business transactions or other business practices in your country and state. Any references to any person or business whether living or dead is purely coincidental.

Every effort has been made to accurately represent this product and it is potential. Examples in these materials are not to be interpreted as a promise or guarantee of earnings. Earning potential is entirely dependent on the person using our product, ideas, and techniques. We do not purport that this is a "get rich scheme."

Your level of success in attaining the results claimed in our materials depends on the time you devote to the program, ideas, and techniques mentioned, plus your finances, knowledge, and various skills. Since these factors differ according to individuals, we cannot guarantee your success or income level. Nor are we responsible for any of your actions.

Any and all forward-looking statements here or on any of our sales material are intended to express our opinion of earnings potential. Many factors will be important in determining your actual results and no guarantees are made that you will achieve results similar to ours or anybody else's, no guarantees are made that you will achieve any results from our ideas and techniques in our material.

All rights reserved worldwide. No part of this book may be reproduced or transmitted in any form whatsoever, electronic or mechanical, including photocopying, recording, or by any informational storage or retrieval without the expressed alert from Calendar written consent of the authors, except for brief excerpts in a review.

Simply 1-2-3 to Success: 3 Steps to Online Marketing Results!

Email: book@simply123tosuccess.com
Website: http://book.simply123tosuccess.com
Copyright © 2021 Nigel Lear

Publication date: 2021

Author: Nigel Lear

ISBN: 9781838535704

All rights reserved. No portion of this book may be reproduced mechanically, electronically, or by any other means, including photocopying, without permission of the publisher or author except in the case of brief quotations embodied in critical articles and reviews. It is illegal to copy this book, post it to a website, or distribute it by any other means without permission from the publisher or author.

Limits of Liability and Disclaimer of Warranty
The author and publisher shall not be liable for your misuse of the enclosed material. This book is strictly for informational and educational purposes only.

Warning – Disclaimer
The purpose of this book is to educate and entertain. The author and/or publisher do not guarantee that anyone following these techniques, suggestions, tips, ideas, or strategies will become successful. The author and/or publisher shall have neither liability nor responsibility to anyone with respect to any loss or damage caused, or alleged to be caused, directly or indirectly by the information contained in this book.

Medical Disclaimer
The medical or health information in this book is provided as an information resource only and is not to be used or relied on for any diagnostic or treatment purposes. This information is not intended to be patient education, does not create any patient-physician relationship, and should not be used as a substitute for professional diagnosis and treatment.

Publishers
10-10-10 Publishing and Independent Publishing Network for United Kingdom
Markham, ON
Canada

Printed in Canada and the United States of America

A catalogue record of this book is available from the British Library.

DEDICATION

I dedicate this book to every person who is opening it with curiosity, open-mindedness, and enthusiasm to understand a little more about online marketing with a simplified approach.

Did you know that 97% of people in internet marketing do not make any money, and that's because they focus on all the wrong things? I get so many great ideas, sometimes too many, but I always focus on one. Remember: Follow One Course Until Success (FOCUS). Stick with me, and this book will show you the right things to focus on: *Simply 1-2-3 to Success.*

"Create your dreams before you consume the work of others." – Nigel Lear

And, of course, I dedicate this book to everyone who helped in its concept and making.

CONTENTS

ACKNOWLEDGEMENTS ix

FOREWORD xi

INTRODUCTION 1

1. WHAT IS ONLINE MARKETING? 5

   Online Marketing Defined 8

   Online Marketing Is Transforming into Content Marketing 11

2. BUILDING YOUR ONLINE BUSINESS 17

   What Are the Digital or Physical Products Available? 19

   What Can I Sell Online? 23

3. BUILD YOUR LIST 27

   What Is a List? 30

   Why Do You Need a List? 31

   Let's Exchange Information 32

4. WHAT IS A NICHE MARKET? 37

   What Is a Niche Market and How Do You Define It? 39

   Identifying Your Influencers 43

5. KNOW YOUR TARGET AUDIENCE 49

   What Is a Target Audience? 51

   How Do You Identify the Target Audience of Your Business? 53

   Getting Reactions from Your Target Audience 57

vii

Contents

6. SET UP SHOP 61

What Is Involved in Setting Up Your Online Business? 66

Building a Product 68

7. KEYWORD RESEARCH 101 73

SEO – What Is It? 79

8. QUICK TRAFFIC GENERATION TACTICS 83

Content Marketing 85

Write Useful Content That Answers a Question 86

Create Evergreen Content 87

Create Long-Form Content 87

Create a List Post 88

Plan Out Content 89

Reuse and Repurpose 90

Connecting with Your Target Audience 91

9. MARKETING OPTIONS—SOCIAL MEDIA AND MOBILE 95

Facebook Marketing 97

Google Advertising and Shopping 101

Social Media Platforms 103

Mobile Marketing 105

10. HAVE THE RIGHT MINDSET 109

What Are the Two Mindsets Driving Leadership? 112

Success or Failure Is a State of Mind 115

Be Creative and Curious 117

ABOUT THE AUTHOR 121

ACKNOWLEDGEMENTS

I would like to thank my friends and family for inspiring me to write this book. This book has been 2 years in the making, 20 months of thought and thinking about it, and 4 months writing the book. It was not clear I'd write this book until I met some inspiring people at a retreat in Cancun last year, which inspired me to complete the book.

"From adversity to strength, connecting the world." – Nigel Lear

Special thanks go to all these people of the Cancun Cluster and Mulberry Hill Gang: Amy Lemire, Charles Tchoreret, Rudi Lickwood, Ani Railkar, Avery Thurman, Emad Saatlou, Marleide Feitosa, Mike Leys, Trish Leys, Paul Wolters, Renee Carlson, Selma Pereira, Stacey Cooper, Charlotte Bonavia, Dan Simon, Fely Castillo David, Rogerio Pereira, Diane Wargalla, Nathalie Sav, Afshien Pour, Bimala Dong Lama, Catherine Carroll, Ursula Pope Garrett, Cathy O, Sophie Polny, Lisa Stringfellow, Nathan Anthony, Miha Bavec, Gregor Hocevar, Natalia Dikun, Lorraine Molley, Ahmed Hawari, Carla Van Wees, Chinmai Swamy, Danielle Privi, Roberta Sengstack, Marsha Shulman, Shirley Neal, Aden Eyob, Olga Dom, Tom Hurley, Olga Kaminer, and Hema Dawonauth.

Finally, with apologies to all those acquaintances and colleagues who may be offended that they have not been named in this acknowledgement (consider yourself in here in spirit if not in print).

FOREWORD

Congratulations on taking the first step toward financial and personal freedom by writing this life-changing book, *Simply 1-2-3 to Success: 3 Steps to Online Marketing Results!*

Within these pages, you will discover the operating instructions for your online success and be offered the key to turn it over and generate profits.

If you tried to replicate this process yourself, amassing all the marketing strategies contained in this book, it would take many years and many thousands of dollars. When you need a vehicle for transportation, you do not build a car from the ground up, do you? While you certainly could, it would take a lot of time, energy, and money. No, you go to the transportation experts — the car manufacturers. In the same way, when you need a vehicle for online marketing and wealth building, you go to the experts at *Simply 1-2-3 to Success*.

Right where you are, you can avoid all the stress that goes with online internet marketing, the pains and financial burden — and just partner with *Simply 1-2-3 to Success: 3 Steps to Online Marketing Results!* You will love the book, as well as their services, online platform, the passion they bring into the partnership, and an awesome community that has taken a CHALLENGE to see you earn an income from your business.

I highly recommend you take this opportunity to benefit both you and your business by reading this book. It will take your online marketing to another level, as it contains the strategies and insights to help you take that quantum leap with online marketing.

Raymond Aaron
New York Times Bestselling Author

INTRODUCTION

Are you seeking financial and personal freedom?

If you are looking for something new in life, something more fulfilling, exciting, or a new path to travel on, you just found it. Sit back, relax, and do not lay this book down until you're finished. It has a magical quality about it.

Do you seek an opportunity that will provide you with a business model that can radically change your living situation, both monetary and otherwise? Because if you are like most people, it is not only financial freedom that you want; it's personal freedom too. Am I right?

But short of winning the lottery, you know it will not just fall into your lap. You will have to work for it; but what if you could structure those working conditions to be the absolute best available? Imagine:

- Unplugging your alarm clock—Your schedule is yours to dictate.

- Tossing the business suits—You wear jeans, t-shirts, and flip-flops to the "office."

- Eliminating the gridlocked commute—You are not a highway hostage anymore.

Knocking off at 2 p.m., 3 p.m., 4 p.m.—anytime you want to do any*thing* you want! No more asking permission for a doctor's appointment, your children's sporting events, a long weekend at the beach, or any other thing you darn well please.

Introduction

Do these working conditions appeal to you? Then I have good news for you. I have created an online business model that allows you to live life on your own terms yet delivers the potential for earnings in excess of your yearly salary in a month.

You can make high-ticket sales and earn hefty commissions without ever having to speak to a customer on the phone, if you do not wish to. I call it an online sales machine because that is really what it is. Once I provide you with the "key," represented by education and training, you simply turn it in the ignition and let the online business model do its job.

What do you bring to this equation? I sum it up with the acronym TEA.

- **Training**

- **Enthusiasm**

- **Application**

You have to get the training to understand how to work the online sales machine. You had to receive training to operate several machines in your life, didn't you? Your automobile, the photocopier at the office, and maybe even a table saw in your workshop—your online sales machine is no different.

You also need to bring enthusiasm. As you begin this endeavor, keep in mind all the things you would like to achieve when you are truly personally and financially free. Let that motivate you toward success.

Lastly, you must apply the training. You have probably heard the old saying, "Knowledge is power." That is a lie. Knowledge is not power. You can know all the mysteries of the universe, and the secrets of success, but if you just sit in your house and watch television, you have nothing. Applied knowledge is where the real power lies. Act on the training by applying it and following the blueprint laid out for you.

The key to your online success is right here in my hand, and I am offering it to you. Do you have the motivation to turn the key and grow a six-figure business, or would you like to stay as you are?

A former mentor of mine used to say, "If you keep doing what you've been doing, you are going to keep getting what you've been getting." If you are happy with the opportunities and income you currently have, by all means keep doing what you have been doing. And, when the parade passes you by and others have snatched the key to the online sales machine from my hand, you can make excuses, blame others, and say, "That could've been me."

I encourage you to take the key from the following pages and learn about this incredible business model. You will learn the steps needed to begin, find the high-ticket products you'll be privileged to sell, the path to follow, and the work you'll need to do, to prosper.

By letting the ideas in this book fill your consciousness, your life will instantly become a fascinating journey. But that journey is not going to begin as if you are walking through an enchanted garden. When you lay this book down, you will be confronted by construction sites, detours, and potholes—in other words, a respectable amount of resistance from virtually everyone you know.

I am speaking from experience. This is not something I have imagined. As you begin to live your dream, you must keep in mind that you are moving in the opposite direction to that which you have been conditioned to follow.

Introduction

I can promise you, if you will permit yourself to get emotionally involved with the ideas that you are about to read, you will get excited. And I mean really excited, dreaming of what you are capable of doing.

Take the key to your online success and turn the page!

"Those who know the truth learn to love it. Those who love the truth learn to live it."

CHAPTER 1

What Is Online Marketing?

The landscape of the world of retail has dramatically changed over the past two decades. Owning a retail business used to mean finding a suitable location, setting up hours, hiring employees, advertising, and studying traffic patterns to determine the likelihood of enough customers to cover your overhead costs while still making a profit. Running a retail business was challenging to say the least.

Today, the landscape of the retail industry has completely changed. Now, retail businesses are less location dependent than they ever were before. In many cases, having a retail business no longer involves a physical location and the costs associated with them. That means building a business can happen with less capital investment and can grow quickly, because you can start small but have your doors open 24 hours a day, seven days a week. How has this dramatic change happened?

The online world has created the platform known as the internet, which makes all this possible. Starting a website, finding the products, and even using fulfilment services means that you simply have to keep your site up to date and answer questions, with the result being that you are building a business and growing your wealth. However, if you have set all that up and are still hearing crickets, then you are finding out that marketing is still critical to the success of your business.

Today's marketing has also shifted away from traditional print and billboard mediums, to online platforms. There are so many ways to reach out to your target audience that were simply never options in the past. Social media, blogs, vlogs, and influencers have become key parts of your marketing strategy. Why?

With social media and online marketing today, you can segment to reach your specific target audience. Simply put, you are getting a greater return on your marketing investment because your ads are reaching the people most likely to click and do business with your company. Throughout these pages, I will be sharing how you can build an online retail business and make it thrive in this exciting new environment.

Before I get into the process of designing your online business, let's talk about online marketing, including what it is and how you can use this tool to positively impact your business.

Online Marketing Defined

To put it simply, online marketing provides a set of tools and methods that you can use to promote products and services throughout the platforms living on the internet. There are a wide range of marketing elements that come into play, simply because the internet offers more avenues and marketing mechanisms for you to reach your target audience.

However, just because you see a business using one online marketing platform, it does not mean that you need to use it. The truth is that the most effective online marketing programs are leveraging consumer data and customer relationship management to build connections and relationships with those that are most likely to convert into paying customers. It wraps your business in a way that traditional advertising could never do. Let's think about it this way.

If you bought a billboard advertising spot for your business, you might put some measures in place to help you determine how successful that billboard was in reaching your customers. That might involve asking customers, when they came in, whether they saw the billboard or if it influenced their decision to come into your business. Even with the best efforts, you are still unlikely

What Is Online Marketing?

to know conclusively the benefits of that billboard in reaching your target audience. Plus, once that billboard campaign ends, you will be gathering data regarding the impact of the message and trying to analyze it. Truthfully, that information is already old. You could adjust the billboard and try again; but again, it will take time for you to get feedback regarding its effectiveness.

Now let's move that same ad to an online platform, such as Facebook. First, you can put your ad onto the platform, and have it targeted to a specific audience, based on the markers that you select. Then you can get feedback right away on how many people are clicking on the ad, watching it, and how many are taking the action to visit your website and make a purchase. If an ad doesn't seem to be doing well, you do not need to wait for weeks or months to make adjustments. They can be made almost instantly, based on your real time analytics. The result is that your marketing can reach your audience where they are at, while making your marketing dollars go even further.

Here are just a few of the advantages that can be found when using online marketing to build your business:

- **Low Costs** – You can reach large audiences for a fraction of the costs that traditional advertising budgets, giving you the ability to create amazing advertising content that appeals to your target market.

- **Flexibility and Convenience** – Your customers are no longer limited to your physical location hours to do their research and have their questions answered when they have the time. It creates a new level of options for your customers to purchase or connect with your business.

- **Analytics** – As I mentioned above, online advertising gives you multiple ways to statistically measure the impact of your online advertising content, without increasing your marketing costs.

- **Multiple Advertising Options** – Instead of being limited to just a few tools or options for your advertising content to be viewed, online platforms allow you to take advantage of a variety of tools. For instance, you can grow your audience organically or take advantage of pay-per-click advertising, email marketing, and even having your business highlighted as part of a local search by those individuals who are looking for businesses using their mobile device, such as Google Maps. These options allow you to be where your target audience is most likely to look for your business.

- **Demographic Targeting** – Advertising dollars are best spent when they reach the people that are most likely to interact with your business and make a purchase. With demographic targeting through online algorithms, you can effectively reach your audience more effectively. Less of your marketing dollars are going to waste as a result.

Clearly, online marketing provides plenty of benefits. Many businesses that started out online have continued to grow to the point that they have reached international status, such as Amazon. However, with all the benefits, there are still some drawbacks that come from having a business online with a focus on advertising primarily on those platforms.

The biggest one is the fact that your potential customers will not be able to pick up and touch your products. That means it might look good on your site but end up being less than a perfect fit for your customers. To counteract that, physical locations are being put in strategic places, allowing individuals to come in and hold the products in their hands.

Apple has done this in a way that gives their customers a variety of ways to interact with their brand. Online, they can check out all the information regarding the product's memory, performance, and more. Then they can go to a local Apple store and actually test-drive the product themselves. Purchases can be made online or right in the store. Online marketing allows for Apple to connect regularly with their customers and build a long-term relationship.

Online Marketing Is Transforming into Content Marketing

As the online platform for businesses continues to grow and change, the shift has gone from creating ads to creating content. The average internet user has put ad blockers in place and made it clear that they do not want to be sold to. Content marketing is a strategic approach to create and distribute valuable, relevant, and consistent content to attract and then retain your targeted demographic, driving positive customer interactions. It is about integrating your content into their everyday lives, particularly on social media.

You are earning their interest with your content, instead of pushing products and services through traditional marketing methods. Today, the internet gives its users the ability to click away from the in-your-face ads. According to a PageFair report[1], 615 million devices are using some form of ad blockers. The use of these ad blockers continues to increase every year. Therefore, content

---

1   https://pagefair.com/blog/2017/adblockreport/

creation is the best way to reach your audience because it is about engaging them, not alienating them.

When you create the content that connects with those individuals, they begin to interact with your company on an organic level. Trust is created, authority established, and connections happen. Loyal followers are easier to convert into sales and leads.

This simple truth has been proven over and over again. YouTube channels are being created by creative individuals, and they are influencing others to connect with brands. The result is an entire industry built around making and sharing content, as well as interacting with individuals regarding that content. What are some of the types of content out there?

- **Blog Posts and Articles** – This is the best way to build a foundation for your content, because you can produce a variety of pages, posts, and content that establishes you as an authority or expert. Plus, all that content can be pointing back to your business and website. Those blogs are also useful to get your content indexed by search engines, helping you to show up in front of the people that you want to lead back to your main website.

- **Infographics** – Think of these graphics as images that can get your point across in a simple and easy to share way. It makes difficult subjects easier to digest and is a fun way to present valuable information to your audience.

- **Case Studies** – This is typically an in-depth overview of some action that your business was able to successfully complete for a client. It is also a great way to showcase how you could perform that similar action for another client dealing with the same challenges. It is also a great way to build trust and expertise.

- **Podcasts** – When it comes to podcasts, you are building an audience in a format similar to radio shows in the past. What makes them popular is the convenience factor, because people can download and listen to them on their timeframe. It can be a great way to share information with your audience, add guest speakers, and cover topics of interest to your target audience.

- **Videos** – If you want to know the hottest form of content right now, it is definitely videos. It is easy to see why they are dominating, because they are easy to consume, often entertain, and appeal to the short attention span of many individuals today. You can build videos for a variety of topics and can incorporate information about your business in a fun way that doesn't feel like a typical forced experience, aka the run-of-the-mill commercial.

While you might already be thinking of several ideas for you to grow your business by creating content in these different areas, the truth is that if you just start creating without a plan, you are going to find it difficult to reach your marketing goals. With that in mind, here are a few strategic points to keep in mind as you start getting creative and building content.

- **Your Brand and Target Audience** – Who are you talking to, and what is your message? Knowing this before you start putting together your content will help you to be appealing to your audience. If you don't target the right audience, then your content is not going to find the traction that you had hoped for.

- **Keywords and Research** – If you know *who* you are targeting, then you have to address *how*. After all, you can create amazing content, but it needs to have the right keywords to get found by the search engines. Doing this research can also help you find natural topics that could be of natural interest to your audience, and which you could incorporate into your content.

- **Plan Your Commitments** – Think about how much time and effort you want to put into your content, and the frequency with which you want to post it. Additionally, determine where you want to post. After all, your target audience is not necessarily on every platform, so you need to choose the one that fits your needs best and focus accordingly.

- **Content Creation** – Here is the point where you take all your research and planning to turn it into content. Spend the time to tweak it. Don't rush just to put it out, because when you do so, the content isn't as good, and it defeats the purpose of posting it in the first place. If you are creating content for multiple platforms, then consider using one piece of content and formatting it to fit the various platforms that you want to post it on.

In the end, creating content and doing all your research is going to mean very little if you cannot combine the content with SEO (search engine optimization) to create significant organic growth. Why is organic growth so important? Simply put, organic growth is free. Having your pages ranked by various search engines can contribute to that organic growth.

As I mentioned earlier, keywords play a part in getting your content ranked. Target keywords should be placed in the headline, titles, meta-description, and sub-headers, as well as the content itself can help the search engines categorize your content effectively.

Later, I will discuss this point in more detail, but for the purpose of online marketing, you also need to make sure that your website is organized and user-friendly. If you have a well-designed site, then it will be more inviting for your audience to stay and interact further with your content. Of course, this is just a simple overview of how SEO works and the importance of keywords in your content.

Now that you have a basic idea of what online marketing is and how it works, let's dive into how you can create a business that maximizes the benefits of online marketing and the social media platforms that support it.

CHAPTER 2

Building Your Online Business

Throughout the first chapter, I introduced you to the amazing world of online marketing and how its impact is continuing to grow on the retail industry. However, as a potential business owner, you might be wondering if starting a business with a viable physical location is worth the effort. Instead, you might be considering creating your business completely online.

I am here to tell you that the future of business is online. Companies with online platforms are selling products and services constantly, and their audience is not limited to one geographical location. Instead, their business is expanding to a global platform, and that is allowing for significant growth. In some cases, the expansion of online business is greater than those businesses with a traditional physical storefront and regular business hours.

You might be thinking, "This is the business route that I want to take." However, at the same time, you don't want to just grab onto any old business. Making the right decisions regarding what you sell online and how you set up your online storefront are critical to building a business that is successful and thriving.

With that in mind, over the next few chapters, I am going to share the tools that I have found successful in building my own online business. This platform can give you the ability to do so much to change your financial trajectory. Now let's get started by discussing the different types of products that can be sold through the online platform.

What Are the Digital or Physical Products Available?

The first thing to recognize is that the online platform provides the opportunity to sell a variety of products. Head out onto your favorite social media platform and you can find literally every type of product, from physical to digital. Do you want to purchase identity theft protection? There is a retailer online that can provide that. Working from home and need a VPN to provide digital security for your home network? There is an online retailer for that.

Looking for more environmentally friendly cleaning products or personal care products? There is an online retailer for that. Whether you are looking for personal products to help care for your loved ones and your home, or digital products that help you to do your job better, including electronics, digital storage, and software, using your favorite search engine, you can find it.

Now, for a moment, let's step back and talk about an industry that has always required you to come to it. The car industry is one where individuals have always had to go to the dealership. That is where you test drive a car, look at the features, negotiate a price, and get financing. Once all those steps have been completed, you get to drive a new (or new to you) car off the lot or forecourt.

How has the online world changed that? Websites offer information about the costs and features of cars, allowing you to do research about everything related to a car. Individuals can find out the mileage per gallon or kilometres per litre. They can do research about the environmental impact of the car's manufacturing process, to how much of an impact it will create once it is on the road.

Around the world, car manufacturers are now offering you the option to digitally build your new car or truck, giving you the ability to choose all the features, the interior, and the color. Once you have made all the choices and agreed to the price, you can order it right online through their platform.

Building Your Online Business

They can even provide financing. However, if you are not ready financially to build a brand-new car, there are options to buy a used car online. That means you can find exactly what you want and make the purchase. The company drops the car off to your home or a specific location, where you walk around and sign off on the condition of the vehicle. Many offer you a 30-day window to drive it and give you the option to return it if there are any mechanical failures.

People have started completing the entire buying process, including research and financing, from their couch. Gone are the days when you had to go to a dealership.

On the other hand, if you are trying to sell your car, it no longer needs to sit on the side of the road with a for-sale sign. You can list it on multiple online platforms or sell it to an online company that buys cars. They will give you an offer and, once you accept, they will request some information and send you paperwork. Once everything is completed, they will come to your home or an agreed upon location, confirm the condition of the vehicle, and then give you a check in exchange for the title and bill of sale.

Even if you decide to use your car for a trade-in at the local dealership, you can come to the dealership armed with information about how much your car is worth as a trade-in, which makes it easier to negotiate.

Does that mean the local car dealership has disappeared? No, but the way they do business has dramatically changed because of the shifting landscape caused by the online platform. Buyers come in armed with research regarding the market value of a vehicle, information about the features they want, and are even prepared with financing, thanks to the fact that banks and credit unions can complete and approve applications done online.

Notice that so much of the pathway to purchase that one product can be completed online. The reason I shared this example is because you need to understand that any product can be sold online. There is no limit.

If you want to sell physical products, there are a variety of options. Today, people are selling cars, houses, and even sports equipment online. Designers are selling their latest clothing options using their website platforms, and even having virtual shows to model their designs.

By the same token, there are plenty of online offerings that you could make available through digital formats. There are plenty of information and entertainment options that can be delivered digitally. Think about eBooks, music, movies, television shows, and more. Then you have other offerings, such as software, subscriptions, and even automated ordering of products, such as personal care items and cleaning supplies.

For example, let's talk about shaving. Men and women both use shaving products in various ways as part of their personal grooming. There are online businesses that have taken advantage of that fact, creating an automated subscription service that sends products and razors to their home every month. The prices are comparable to what they might have paid by going to the store and shopping for these items themselves, but with the subscription service, they are getting convenience. Many of these online businesses take advantage of the fact that people want one less thing to worry about and sell themselves as the solution.

You can likely think of many other examples that fall into this category. Membership sites are continuing to grow. Other individuals have started making money with the creative content that they are making for various social media platforms. As their popularity grows, then businesses want to advertise with these individuals and connect with the community that they have built.

Then there are the websites that create content and capture data that turns into leads for other businesses. Insurance brokers, for instance, actually collect leads through their online content and then shop those leads to insurance companies, helping them connect with individuals who are looking to make a change in their insurance coverage.

Today, the way the online platform is set up, individuals who create quality content can draw affiliate offers to provide to their communities. There might be a podcast you enjoy, or an individual who makes funny videos. All of them are building communities that they sell access to by means of an affiliate program. If you purchase an item through their link, then they make money from a percentage of your purchase. Many of these affiliate offers provide a small discount to their community, but the hope is that they will continue to do business with them once they get access to their products and services.

Notice that all of these options give you multiple chances to use your network or community to build up your business. It can be hard work to get started, but as those individuals on YouTube and other platforms can attest, there are plenty of opportunities to use content creation to build a steady stream of income.

With all that in mind, let's talk about what you might want to sell online.

What Can I Sell Online?

The truth is that the only limit to what you can sell online is your own interests and imagination. There are literally so many possibilities out there.

Book.Simply123ToSuccess.com

As I discussed throughout the earlier parts of this chapter, those options are not limited to physical products but can also include selling digital options as well.

At this point, I also want to talk about the fact that you can build an online business by providing specific services to other businesses. Think about how many small or medium businesses want to increase their presence on social media, but simply do not have the skills or the time. If you have those marketing skills, you could build a business around the process of helping other business owners promote themselves, their products, and their services.

In other cases, you can take your experience and knowledge, packaging it into courses that can help others learn the skills that you have developed over time. Throughout my time in exploring marketing and learning how businesses grow, I have developed multiple courses discussing a variety of the topics related to growing your business online.

Here are just a few of the options that I have offered:

- Video marketing
- Building a brand
- Market research
- Understanding the importance of keywords
- Social media platforms
- Traffic strategies for lead generation
- Building sales funnels and sales pages
- SEO – Search Engine Optimization

Building Your Online Business

These are just a few of the courses and educational opportunities that I offer. I saw a problem or gap in the services available to business owners and stepped in with offerings that created a solution. Perhaps the type of online business that you create could do something similar.

What I found as I created my business is that there are 3 simple marketing steps to follow, and by doing so, I was able to successfully start and grow my online business. These 3 steps can work for you as well. They can help you to leverage all the online tools available to increase the size of your audience, and also increase the likelihood that you will be able to get them to take the step of purchasing your products or services.

These steps are part of a number of methods and techniques that I have learned over the years. My aim is to help you take the steps and use them to achieve more with online marketing as part of the process of building your business. In Chapter 1, I focused on exploring what was possible with online marketing. Now let's jump into the first step, which involves building your list.

CHAPTER 3
Build Your List

No matter what idea you have or business you want to pursue, it will not be successful without the right market or customer base. After all, you can create something amazing, but it will not be able to thrive without the income that results from sales. Time and again, online businesses need to connect with those individuals that want or need the solutions and services that they are offering.

If you are ready to venture into the world of an online business, then you are likely looking for a way to connect with those individuals in the online world. Today's customers are not finding out about products and services in traditional ways, such as through media and print. Instead, they are on various social media platforms, being introduced to products and services by influencers, their friends and family, and the algorithms that power the world of social media.

While it means that you can get more targeted in your marketing than ever before, it also brings up challenges when it comes to grabbing their attention. Your business is competing with millions of other businesses for the time, attention, and most importantly, the money of these customers. If they choose another business over yours, then you lost an opportunity to grow that relationship and capture a sale.

Online marketing is meant to help you spread the message, capture their interest, and lead them to your website, where you can use your products, services, and call to action to create a sale. However, in this chapter, I want to focus more on how you build a list by defining your audience and then creating opportunities for them to connect with you and your business. First, let's start by talking about what a list is, why it is necessary, and then how you create one.

Book.Simply123ToSuccess.com

What Is a List?

When it comes to marketing in today's internet focused and tech-driven world, you can't simply hope that individuals are going to be drawn to your business through word of mouth or traditional marketing platforms. In fact, that type of thinking will likely end up sinking your business. Why? Because today's online businesses need to know something about their audience. Most traditional marketing platforms hire advertising but can only give you estimates about how many people you reached, who they were, and if they fell within your primary audience or secondary audience.

Your list is made up of the characteristics of your target market, as well as a physical list of your customer base. The combination helps you to understand who you are targeting in your content and marketing, as well as giving you the tools to build relationships with your audience.

Now you can define your target audience and its characteristics, and then find the platforms where they are most likely to be found. If you are offering products and services related to crafting, for instance, then you would look to connect with them on Pinterest or Instagram. Your list is going to include information about your target audience. Here are a few examples to consider:

- What do they like?

- Where do they hang out online?

- What type of podcasts or videos do they tend to watch?

- Are your products or services more gender or age specific?

- Are you appealing to families, retirees, or single people just starting out?

Build Your List

The reason you want to know this information is because the more you define your target audience, the easier it will be to choose the platforms and content to appeal to them. Your list helps you to clearly define who you are looking to connect with, both as your primary audience and your secondary ones.

Never discount that secondary audience. While they might not be your primary focus, you can easily pick up the sales to justify targeting them from time to time. I want to be clear that building your list is about getting yourself into the minds of your audience, understanding who they are, and then taking that information and using it to choose the right platforms to advertise on. Another aspect of your list is going to be your actual customer list, but more about that later.

Why Do You Need a List?

One of the reasons that you need a list is because without it, you are advertising blindly. Your resources and capital are not being used effectively in terms of the sales generated. Essentially, it is as if you are placing a billboard out at the side of the road and hoping your customers are going to stop into your business.

Having an online business means you are not dealing with the traditional overhead, but you are still faced with the challenges that come with building sales. Having a list allows you to target your resources more effectively to reach the largest number of individuals within your target audience. Once you have that list, you can broadcast to them through multiple platforms, sharing information to teach them about your products, and hopefully have them turn to your business when they are ready to buy.

Remember, all this work is helping you better understand who you want to target and why. Once you start digging in and doing the research, you might find that who you want to serve is not exactly who you thought it was. On the other hand, you might have a better idea of how your products or services can be used more effectively as a solution to address a problem or need.

As I discuss your niche in the next chapter, having your list will help you determine the right niche to focus on, versus choosing a random one that ultimately doesn't fit your target audience. Now that you have built your marketing list, understanding the criteria of your target customer, then you are ready to start determining how you are going to connect with them.

That leads me to one of my favorite aspects of list building, and that is figuring out the best way to connect with that target audience; and on to one of the critical aspects of building your list, which is gathering information to build a customer list.

Let's Exchange Information

One thing that successful businesses have learned to do is to capture your information. The plan is that by getting your contact information, they can then use that to keep in contact, letting you know about their latest offerings, newest products, or even just what they are doing in the face of challenging circumstances, such as a natural disaster or pandemic.

Their goal is to build a relationship with you by continuing to connect with you, providing information, interesting content, and more. Over time, they hope that when you are ready to make a purchase, they will be the company you think of first, and that you end up spending money with them. Larger companies can use their physical sales force to capture that information.

Let's take a retailer in the mall or shopping center. They might ask for things like your email address or phone number. The goal is to build a list that allows them to direct content to you. It might be a simple monthly or weekly newsletter, but over time, as they collect information about what you click on and the articles that you spend the most time reading, they can begin to customize the content to your interests.

You might be thinking to yourself that it sounds like a lot of work. While it does take effort, the truth is that often one piece of content can be repurposed to serve as content across multiple platforms. However, I want you to get into the mentality that you are going to collect contact information and build a following, because that is going to help you grow your customer base. Here are a few ways to get started in building that content list:

Ask them to join your newsletter or mailing list – When someone visits your website, they are showing an interest in your business. You want to capitalize on that. Ask for contact information and be clear about why you want it. Let them know what they will be receiving in exchange, be it e-coupons, exclusive offers, or newsletters. Once they join, you can start building your relationship. But be warned. It can be easy to start overwhelming them with contact, so it is important to balance between content to build a relationship and overdoing to the point that they put you into their spam or junk folder.

Encourage them to follow you on social media – One of the ways that you can also build your list is through your various social media platforms. How many times have you followed someone, and had them ask you to follow them on Instagram, Facebook, or Twitter, the top main three? Clearly, the point is to give them more opportunities to grow their audience. You can follow their example. Why do you want an online following? Because they are naturally going to share, comment on, and draw attention to your content. Once they do, then others see your content, and the cycle continues to organically grow your audience.

Join panels or podcasts that have the audience you want – If you can be a guest speaker on a panel or podcast, you are introducing yourself to your target audience. Think of it this way. That podcast or panel has already captured your audience, so you will be giving them useful information about your industry or product. It grows your credibility with them, allowing you to be viewed as an authority. Truthfully, you can also give them your contact information, allowing you to capture a chunk of your target market through one guest appearance.

Consider a paid boost of your content – The truth is that social media platforms throughout the internet provide ways for your business to build an audience organically. However, that can take time, often putting you in the position of not being able to grow your business as fast as you would like. However, many of these social media platforms also provide the means to bring you right to your target audience through their advertising platforms. That means a post or content can be put into the newsfeeds of those individuals that fit your target audience parameters, thus allowing you to connect with more people in a shorter time frame. The benefit is that this can be cost-effective, especially for newer online businesses that are just starting out. Once you get in front of your target audience and grab their attention, it is up to you to create the content, as well as offer the services and products that will keep their attention.

Find an influencer – Another way to build your list is by using an influencer and having them talk about your product. There are subscription services or specific products that are raved about on social media by celebrities and content creators. Those individuals drive their audience to your product and allow you to increase your audience and build your list.

Note that everything I am doing is driving toward building an audience, a customer base, and allowing them to share my business with their social media networks. I want to point out that many of the aspects of your list building are going to happen alongside your product research, defining your niche, and doing research on your target audience. No list is ever finished. In fact, more often than not, your list will continue to be refined, as your business changes, your product line matures, and your definition of your target audience gets clearer.

While this part of your journey might seem to involve a lot of studying, compiling information, and more, the truth is that you will be grateful for the time you took to build a list. Simply put, that list will help you to grow your repeat business, simply because you will have connected with them and now put yourself in the position to keep building that relationship.

However, before you can truly build a list, you need to understand your target audience, and that means knowing your niche so that you can define your target audience. Let's get started!

CHAPTER 4

What Is a Niche Market?

One of the critical parts of building any business is understanding who you are marketing to and their characteristics. The truth is that you can have an amazing product or idea, but if you are targeting the wrong audience, then your business is likely to fall flat. Still, you might be wondering how you can define the audience for your particular product or service. There might be a few clues in the product or service itself that helps to narrow it down slightly.

How can you narrow it down even further? The journey starts by defining your niche market. First, before you can do that, it is important to know what a niche market is.

What Is a Niche Market and How Do You Define It?

In the broadest possible terms, a niche market is a subset of a larger market that has its own unique needs or preferences. The result is that you have a uniquely defined group that stands out underneath a larger umbrella group. Let's think of it this way. Women's shoes are a large market, but within that market, there are a variety of niche markets. For example, there are shoes for women who work in the medical field, shoes for plus-sized women, or shoes that appeal to environmentally conscious consumers.

Each of those types of shoes are appealing to a unique group of women within the larger marketplace. Therefore, depending on the type of shoes that you are creating for women, you would want to get to know the preferences or unique needs of the women in those sub-groups or niches.

The truth is that every group, no matter how narrow you set the parameters, can be divided down even further by the needs and preferences of those within that group. Here are just a few ways to define a niche market:

- **Price** – Different groups are going to be drawn to a product based on price. For some, the price might indicate a higher quality or prestige associated with the product or service. However, being at a lower price point can attract bargain hunters and those who are budget conscious. Therefore, depending on how you want your product to be perceived by your niche market, your price point can play a key in attracting that set of target consumers.

- **Demographic Base** – These are the broad factors found in most marketing campaigns. Defining a niche often starts by figuring out the basic demographic information about your target audience, such as gender, age, income level, and education completed.

- **Level of Quality** – As mentioned above, the level of quality of your product is going to play a part in defining your niche market. For instance, a high-quality product with a higher price point attracts a different niche than someone who might be willing to settle for slightly less quality to have a cheaper price. Most people are not going to discount chains looking for high quality items at a discounted price. Designers also add prestige to their products with a higher level of quality, building in the idea that those products are worth more because of the designer and the materials they choose to use.

- **Psychographics** – This area might be slightly harder to quantify, but it is possible to break down a target audience even further by their values, interest, and attitudes. Let's use sustainability and the environment as an example. Your product or service might cost more, but your customers are willing to pay that because it aligns with their beliefs and attitudes regarding the environment. However, someone who is focused on price points, because their values and beliefs align with saving money, might not be as willing to purchase that same product or service. At the same time, you do not want to fall victim to the idea that if someone is looking for a good deal, they are not interested in the environment or taking other aspects of the product or service into consideration. Often, this area of understanding your niche market is about recognizing which value or belief is likely to be the priority in their decision making regarding a purchase.

- **Geographical** – While knowing information about where your target niche market is physically located can be critical in determining where you want to put a bricks and mortar store, the truth is that for an online business, this is not as critical since you can market to a wide group of individuals through an online platform. Still, having an idea of where your niche market is concentrated can help you to develop a marketing strategy to target specific countries, states, or counties for your advertising and social media posts.

As you can see, the process of defining a niche involves learning about your target customer and doing research to narrow down their specific needs and wants. Even though it takes some initial effort to define your niche, once you do so, marketing to that niche can be much easier, because they have more in common regarding wants, preferences, and needs.

When you understand the different needs of your niche market, then you can speak very specifically to those needs in your marketing. That specific messaging will give you a greater chance of attracting your customer's attention and getting them into your sales funnel. Here are just a few of the benefits that come from targeting a specific niche market:

- **Reduced Competition** – The truth is that the broader your target audience, the greater your competition for their attention. However, once a niche market is shown to be profitable, recognize that others may try to move into that space. Still, if you are the first to that niche market, then you will set the standard for the competition to follow.

- **Focused Business Tactics** – The reality is that a narrower audience allows you to be focused on addressing specific customer needs and wants, instead of trying to spread your marketing resources over a larger market.

- **Providing Expertise** – Identifying your niche market also gives you the opportunity to become known as a specialist within your industry. With an expert reputation, your niche market is likely to come to your business based on its reputation and experience.

- **Create a Chance for Expansion** – By clearly identifying your niche market, you can expand into new markets, simply because you would be able to identify other needs or preferences that they have and develop products or services to meet them.

The trick of finding the right niche market is to look for a segment that has needs you can meet and also the ability to grow over time. There are a variety of products that meet a need, but they end up being just a flash in the pan, and the business fizzles out simply because it cannot grow.

As you try to build your niche, it is important to think about what your product or service offers, the needs it meets, and then build a target customer based on that information. Too often, people identify a niche market, only to find that there are not enough customers to make it viable, or that there is not enough of a market for long-term growth. Therefore, if you find that your niche is too small, be open to expanding your product line or even exploring another product or service altogether.

The goal is to determine the niches that already exist and explore where niches can expand profitably. By meeting the demands of a given audience through specialization, communication with your target customers, and providing a quality experience, then you are going to build the reputation necessary to grow within your identified niche.

Identifying Your Influencers

Throughout the process of identifying your niche, a few key aspects are going to stand out. Those keys are going to lead you to various influencers. What is an influencer?

In the world of online marketing, an influencer has built a relationship with their audience, influencing that audience's purchases based on the influencer's experience and knowledge. Various influencers tend to create a relationship with a distinct niche audience, and they often engage with that audience through various social media outlets.

YouTube is a great example of influencers at work. Many of them build an audience and then market various products to them, either through defined sponsor relationships or a partnership with a brand that focuses on achieving their marketing objectives.

How they build their audience also gives them the social relationships necessary to be trusted when they present products or services to their audience. Any brand loves social media influencers, simply because they can often be the starting point of a trend that leads their audiences to purchase their promoted products.

Now, before you start thinking that you can just work with any particular individual who claims to be an influencer with your niche audience, you need to know about the types of influencers out there.

- **Mega-influencers** – These are the people who have the largest numbers of followers, typically over the 1 million range on at least one social media platform, although they can have that large number of followers across multiple social media platforms. Think celebrities and others who actually got famous and built an audience in the real world before transitioning to an online audience. The truth is that much of their online audience is actually made up of those fans or followers that know them for their original celebrity status, not necessarily their online activities. However, this is not always the case, because some mega-influencers have built an online audience and created their own celebrity on that platform. Unfortunately, these mega-influencers are basically only available to major brands because they can be costly to work with. They may have an agent who you need to approach regarding a marketing deal. Expect that mega-influencers are going to naturally be fussy

What Is a Niche Market?

about who they work with, because it can impact the trust they have with their following.

- **Macro-influencers** – These influencers are just under the mega-influencers, with a range of followers from 40,000 to 1 million. Now, they might be B-list celebrities, the ones that aren't quite famous enough to be considered a mega-influencer. Others are building online celebrity, using their knowledge and expertise to grow an audience. They can help you to raise awareness of your brand and build a following of your own within your niche market. A word of caution if you choose to work with one of these influencers, as it could be less that they built the audience organically but bought it.

- **Micro-influencers** – These are not celebrities who have a large following due to their work in different arenas. In fact, they are often just ordinary people who build their following based on their unique knowledge or expertise. Keep in mind that their numbers of followers can vary from 1,000 to more, but the really critical part is the relationships they have built and the interactions they have with their followers through the different social media platforms they use. What is interesting is that these ordinary people are building a celebrity of their own, and that celebrity has translated into other opportunities for them. Consider these influencers the ones that will be critical in the future. The reason is that everything is getting fragmented even more, thanks to social media. So even if your niche is rather small, there is still a Facebook group or other gathering spot on social media for these individuals to get together. If they are getting together online, then there are influencers growing within these groups.

- **Nano-influencers** – If you are looking for an influencer in a highly specialized area, then these are the ones you are looking to connect with. If your product or service falls into a specialized niche, then these are the influencers that you are likely going to try to tap. However, to reach a broad audience, you would need too many of these nano-influencers to make it an effective marketing option.

All of these influencers are making use of social media platforms in a variety of ways. They might be a regular blogger, combining journalism with their opinions of different products and services. Think of mothers who speak about their challenges and experiences through their blogs, building an audience because they are funny, truthful, or have a way of pointing out the absurd. Other bloggers specialize in personal development, health, music, and so many other topics that I couldn't list them all. Suffice it to say, pretty much any product, service, or interest has a blog being written about it somewhere by someone.

If a blog has enough influence, you might be able to buy a sponsored post on their website, or even write a guest blog that gives you an opportunity to highlight your product or services. The key here is that you have to align with the core message of the blog, or the audience is not going to be influenced to consider exploring your products any further. Another point to keep in mind is that Gen Z is used to this type of marketing, so they won't be turned off by a sponsored post most of the time.

However, you might be wondering if blogs are the only tools available to an influencer. The truth is, that is furthest from the truth. Videos and audio are growing in popularity. Influencers can build an audience discussing topics that appeal to that niche audience or are based on how current events could be impacting them. One of the things I want to point out here is that getting to know the content of influencers can give you a deeper insight into your niche audience. It can also give you ideas of how you could expand your core business beyond your initial offerings.

While they are creating all this content, these influencers are not just hoping that individuals will stumble upon it. Instead, they are using social media posts to draw attention to their content. Thus, many of them end up making a name on social media that leads their audience to their other work.

Picking an influencer can be challenging, because while they might be a celebrity, those influencers might lack credibility with your target audience. Plus, celebrities might not want to be known as a marketing channel, making them less willing to get involved in an influencer campaign. To be fair, these celebrities might also lack any actual influence over their customers.

Depending on your niche, it might be better to use a key opinion leader because of the respect they have earned. You are piggybacking off their reputation. If you get the ear of a journalist, and they mention your company or product, then you have received the benefits of an influencer outside of a blog or social media influencer. Another plus is that these mentions are likely to be free but provide a boost to your brand's profile within your niche.

Still, finding influencers and building a niche audience means that you have a deeper understanding of who your target audience is, where they can be found online, and how you can connect with them. Let's start moving in that direction by getting into what your target audience might look like, based on the niche that you defined throughout this chapter.

CHAPTER 5

Know Your Target Audience

Finding your target audience is critical to the growth of your business. No matter how good the idea or amazing the product, if you don't have customers, your business will be unable to make money, plain and simple. However, if you have been in business a while, your target audience may have shifted from what it was when you first started out.

On the other hand, a new business needs to have an idea of that target audience before they even open the doors. In either case, even after your target audience is identified, you still need to be open to adjusting as you learn more about who is buying your products and services. Still, before you can market to your target audience, you need to know what it is and who belongs in that group.

What Is a Target Audience?

The simplest definition of a target audience is the group of people that you are making your products and services for. You might have heard terms like "target market" or "target customer" as well. All these terms basically mean the same thing. Here are a few examples of businesses and target audiences.

- **Lawn care service** – Homeowners within a specific mile radius, taking care of yards or landscaping

- **Yoga professional** – Adults or children interested in learning or practicing the art of yoga

- **Graphic designer** – Businesses with high-end products and services

If you are just starting out in business, there is the temptation to just get started selling and not worry about whether or not you have defined that target audience. That is a mistake, especially in an online retail environment where marketing can be so detailed and precise. Another reason to know your target audience is the fact that online marketing involves creating content. You can't possibly understand what type of content will appeal to your target audience if you don't know who they are.

Creating marketing materials that are appealing to a target audience has always been a challenge for businesses. Before the internet allowed us to define so precisely the type of individuals that we wanted to show our ads to, marketing was a broader industry. You put up a commercial during a time slot when you were most likely to reach your target audience, but there were no guarantees. It was an educated shot in the dark.

Digital marketing has changed all that. Now there are ways to reach a specific customer down to the very smallest details. However, your business doesn't benefit if you are not able to initially define your target audience and then refine that as you receive more information. Much of that refining will come from your sales data as you learn more about your specific customer type. Knowing your target audience clearly will impact a variety of things, including:

- Your price points
- Your product or service offerings
- Keywords used in your marketing materials and content
- Your overall design
- When you advertise
- Where you advertise
- What you will highlight in your content and marketing materials

There are a variety of benefits to your business plan if you know who your target audience is and what they want or need. Well, that is great, you might be thinking, but how do I actually identify that target audience?

How Do You Identify the Target Audience of Your Business?

There are a variety of characteristics that you need to focus on as you are figuring out what your target audience looks like. In sharing a few of these, I want to get you thinking about the products and services you want to offer, and who they are most likely to relate to. Recognize that research might be necessary. The truth is that you can often be surprised by who you originally thought might be interested in your products and services, and what the research ends up telling you.

- **Demographics** – This information is the most basic outline of your target audience. It typically involves age, gender, income, marital status, occupation, and educational level. These can give you broad groups, and then you can use additional information to narrow it down even further.

- **Psychographics** – This data can be trickier, simply because it involves getting to know personality types, likes, and dislikes. You often can't figure it out based on the demographics you have already collected. That means you need to start collecting information based on interests, activities, hobbies, attitudes, and opinions. Polls are one way to figure out where your demographics and psychographics match up.

Remember, the goal of gathering this data is to help you figure out where your target audience is spending their time online, how often they are online, and what type of content is most likely to appeal to them. I would argue you that while you might be able to gather some of this information before you start putting out content, it is your social media posts and content that will help you to refine your target audience even further. After all, you are getting feedback from perspective customers about what they liked and what they didn't. Common marketing wisdom is to pick at least two identifiers from both demographics and psychographics, because it will help you to narrow down your target audience without making it so narrow that you are struggling to find individuals who fit into that group.

Now, you might be wondering how you can grow your understanding of your target audience. After all, you initially created a target audience with broad strokes, but now you want to get more specific. The truth is that your target audience might not be spending much time on Facebook, but if you are putting a majority of your content on that platform, then you are not connecting with that target audience.

That is why I believe in getting familiar with the various tools available on social media platforms meant to assist you in growing your understanding of your target audience. Let's explore this type of tool on the largest social media platform, Facebook.

Facebook Audience Insights provides a way to select different audience criteria, then learn the size of your target market, and trends related to that market. The criteria can include location, demographics, and even behaviors. Here is a simple example of how this tool can benefit your business. Say you want to open a business focusing on making candles. Facebook Audience Insights gives you the option to choose women and an age range. It will then give you an estimate of the size of that market. You will also get additional information about that target market, which can be key in your understanding of what they want from your business and how you can best serve them. Once you have that understanding, crafting marketing materials and content can be simpler.

A word of caution with using this tool from Facebook: Most of the information gathered is based on self-reported data and the tracking of individual behaviors on the platform. That means if your target audience is not using Facebook, then these insights might not serve you as well. Again, it boils down to having those broad strokes of a target audience, which will help you figure out the best marketing tools to use as part of defining that audience even further.

Google is one of the biggest search engines in the world and, with that, they have collected billions of pieces of information about how people use the internet, their interests, what they buy, the social media platforms they use—and the list could go on and on. Businesses often use Google to get their business noticed on maps and other tools, available to those who extensively use the search engine. However, businesses are also finding it a useful place to learn more about their target audience and give them additional platforms to connect.

Google Trends is just one of the marketing tools that Google makes available. There are also tools that help you see how your posts are rating, how your website rates in searches, and more. The focus of Google Trends is to determine the interest in various keywords over time. Once you type in a keyword, then you are going to get information about when that keyword is most frequently searched, and the areas where those searches are most prevalent.

Can you imagine being able to target your content to specific areas during specific times of the year, increasing the likelihood of reaching your target audience when they are most interested in making a purchase? Essentially, Google's tools give you some incredible insights into how your target audience behaves over a longer period, based on the data they gather.

Another useful tool is Claritas MyBestSegments, where you can look up specific zip codes within the United States and find out the common market segments within that area. There is also other demographic information available, but if you are building an internet business, then limiting your demographic information to one country or geographical area could mean you are missing your target audience, simply because you are ignoring their location.

This tool can also be used to search by market segment and pick-up information about behavior, financial behavior, and even the type of technology they are using. Why would you want to know about the technology that your target audience is using?

Imagine creating amazing content, which is best viewed on a desktop, yet your target market is primarily using their mobile devices, where your content does not show well. They are not staying to watch your content, and you are missing an opportunity to connect with them. Knowing your target market's technology preferences can be key to tailoring your content for the platforms and devices they use the most often.

If it feels like you are drowning in data right now, then you probably are. The best way to start determining what you can drop and what you should focus on is by interacting with your target audience. How is that possible?

Getting Reactions from Your Target Audience

With all the demographic information that you have, there might be a few people you can identify who seem to fit. Reach out to them and talk with them about your product or services. Use this opportunity to get their thoughts, including finding out if they have purchased similar products or services in the past. Here are a few questions to help you gather their feedback:

- What are their major concerns with similar products and services?

- Would they purchase those products and services again?

- How satisfied were they with their previous experiences?

- Did they have any reservations or issues that your business could solve, thus making them more likely to use your business?

The answers to these questions can give you indications of whether you are on the right track with defining your target audience, or if you are still off base and need to do some additional refining. However, if you are creating a new product or service for your internet business, you might not have immediate contacts who fit into your target audience.

Again, you are building an internet business, so reaching out to the internet for feedback is a great option. Think about the millions of different groups on social media platforms that cover a variety of interests, demographics, and more. Search for the groups that seem to closely match your target audience definition, and then connect with them. Use the same questions to start a discussion and get feedback. Marketing means getting feedback, adjusting, and putting it out there again for more feedback.

Perhaps your business has already gotten some positive feedback and you have built a few connections, starting a critical contact list with emails. Now use that email list to send out a mock-up of your latest product or service. Is there interest from your list in that product? Then consider moving forward. If it does not generate any buzz, then you can retool it and try again.

There are multiple ways to build an email list, and much of that I covered in Chapter 3. Right now, I want you to recognize that there are multiple ways to connect with your target market to get the feedback necessary to see if you are on track or if you need to go back and adjust the parameters for your target market.

Even when you start selling your products or services, your target market might be refined, or you might find that another market jumps out as a way to expand your business even further. One of the benefits of online marketing is that your adjustments can be made quickly, because feedback on content can happen within a short window of time. Think about how traditional marketing meant waiting for feedback over weeks or months.

While it might be tempting to start buying ads right away, the truth is that you could be wasting valuable capital without reaching your target audience. Doing the work outlined in this chapter is key to defining your marketing plan, building content, and purchasing ads on the right platforms. Once you know the needs and interests of your target audience, then it makes defining that marketing plan easier.

The other benefit is that it can tweak your products and services. After all, if they are interested but tell you about things they would prefer, you may find it helps to make those adjustments and boost your sales in the process.

Know Your Target Audience

The truth is that once you start acting on your marketing plan based on that target audience, it may turn out that your target market will change. That is normal. Undeserved markets will also start to be identified. Offers can demonstrate whether your target market is responding. If they are not, then offers can be changed, or you might alter what your target market looks like and try it again.

Up to this point, the groundwork has been laid for your online business. You have identified a product or service that easily fits the online platform, built a list, found a niche market, and gotten to know your target audience. With that foundation in place, now it is time to set up shop and start creating your product or service.

Over the next few chapters, let's dive into that process, as well as the importance of keywords, traffic generation tactics, the various marketing options available, and the trends in online marketing with the increasing use of mobile devices by different market segments.

CHAPTER 6
Set Up Shop

At this point, you know your target audience, have an idea, and are excited to get started. The beauty of using an online store platform is that your start-up costs are relatively low, especially if you are delivering a digital product. That being said, I want to focus on choosing a product and setting up shop. Learning about your target audience is going to help you better define your product offerings. First, let's go back a bit to your niche market and how you can use what you learned to help you better determine the type of product you want to produce, as well as how that can impact your online business.

As you were thinking about your niche market, here are three characteristics that should have popped up. They have money to spend, they have an ongoing desire or interest (meaning they could be a repeat customer), and they can be found online. In Chapter 4, I discussed niche markets in depth, along with how influencers play a part in building a niche audience.

Now that you are ready to set up shop, it is important to know whether the niche market you have decided on has longevity. For instance, internet dating has a monthly search volume of over 5 million, and there are over 183 million dating sites in Google. Can you imagine that this niche market is going away any time soon?

The goal is to find or develop such a niche market for yourself. Where can you find some niche ideas of your own? Here are a few places where you might find some niche ideas:

- Your job
- Any ideas that pop into your head
- Areas of your expertise
- Hobbies and interests

- Friends and family

- Conversations

The truth is that niche ideas can pop up in your everyday interactions with various social media forums, triggered by books or articles in newspapers and magazines, or even television and radio. Why are these great places to get inspired? Simply because these are avenues that expose you to the challenges and needs of your potential target audience.

When you identified a target audience, you essentially created the wish list of people that you want to do business with, by identifying specific characteristics. For example, you might be creating a gaming solution that could be appealing to teenagers. However, teenagers are a broad definition, but teenagers in a family with a specific income level is narrowed and more precise.

While it might be tempting to choose a broad niche, the truth is that you cannot appeal to everyone. There is no product that is truly one-size-fits-all. Still, you might be looking for niches in some of the areas above and coming up blank. Another option is to focus on your interests, experience, and skills. For instance, you might have spent a number of years consulting, but also working for a small business. Therefore, you might combine them to create a consulting company focused on serving small businesses.

Now you have a target audience, perhaps a few ideas of how to serve them, and an understanding of the skills and experience that you can offer them. As you bring all these parts together, your niche begins to emerge. A niche is going to take on five qualities, regardless of what it is:

- It takes you in the direction that you want to go.

- Customers are interested.

- You have carefully planned your approach to getting your target audience's interest.

- It is one of a kind, something that serves a need being missed by other companies in the industry.

- It is capable of evolving to create different profit centers, while still meeting the needs of the core business.

All of these qualities are going to help you create a long-term sustainable business. Use these criteria to evaluate the ideas that you have already come up with. Perhaps you have an idea that is exciting, but it will mean that you have to do more travel than you planned. The result of your evaluation means your idea does not meet all of the five qualities mentioned above and, therefore, might not be the right fit for you.

At this point, you have likely identified a niche market and perhaps a product or service that you can provide digitally or through a physical shipment. Now it is time to test that product with your target audience. Earlier, I discussed testing a product or niche market to see if it is actually viable. Now you can move to the next level by offering your product for sale, using samples, or even offering a free download of one aspect of your product or service.

Think of businesses that offer free items. Often, it is a way to connect with potential customers, allowing them the opportunity to explore your offerings further. As you test, keep in mind that you are not trying to spend a fortune. Instead, you are focused on determining the level of interest for what you are offering. For instance, if you offer a mini seminar demonstrating your consulting skills, and you have few nibbles, then it might mean you need to tweak what you are offering to your niche market in order to grab their interest.

Book.Simply123ToSuccess.com

I have seen online businesses rise and fall simply because they thought the idea was good enough, but the reality was that it did not have much backing or opportunities for growth. Now, at this point, you are dipping your toes into market research. Every test gives you feedback and allows you to adjust. With all this effort to find your niche and determine the product or service that fits your target market, it has left you with multiple ideas.

What Is Involved in Setting Up Your Online Business?

Right at this moment, you are probably excited to get started. That energy is driving you to act, but the actual process of setting up a business can be overwhelming.

- Do you set up a legal entity?
- How do you set up a legal entity?
- How do you get your product made, shipped, and delivered?
- How do you accept payment?
- How do you create a marketing plan?

The list of questions can go on and on. For an online business, I always get my clients focused on taking tangible steps, thus allowing them to avoid getting overwhelmed. One of the first things you need to do is set up a legal entity for your business. Doing so will allow you to separate the finances of your business from your personal finances.

Doing so means you now have a legal business, giving you various protections under the laws of your country, and may keep you in compliance.

In the European Union (EU), creating a legal business means that you need to make sure that you are following the General Data Protection Regulation (GDPR) and maintaining your compliance. What is that?

In April 2016, the EU adopted the GDPR, which introduces new obligations to data processors and data controllers, with the focus on data privacy. There are multiple areas that you need to be aware of as you set up your online business. One of the most important requirements is that you need to get explicit consent from your customers and those visiting your website regarding how their data is being used. They also have the right to request that aspects of their data be held or deleted.

As part of creating your website, you need to put specific data processes in place to comply with getting consent, and also make sure that your data is not being used in other ways than what was consented to. It will also play a part in the security and encryption measures that you put into place on your website.

Next, it is time to get a domain name and hosting platform. After all, you are building an online business, and this step is the equivalent of finding a physical retail location. In line with the GDPR, your hosting platform needs to give you the flexibility to put the elements in place that keep you in compliance.

The reason this is critical is because the internet allows you to gain customers from many locations, including the EU. Therefore, if you have European customers, then you must comply with this law and its requirements. I am here to tell you that it is easier to build these elements into your platform from the beginning, versus trying to put them into place retroactively.

There are a variety of tools out there to assist you in this process. I consult with businesses regularly and give guidance on how to navigate the GDPR. At this point, I also want to note that while the EU has taken the lead on privacy and data security in this regard, other countries and states are creating laws with a similar ideology behind them. If your business is not in one of these countries or states, you might think that you do not have to worry about it. The truth is that this trend is likely to continue, so being proactive can be a potentially cost-saving measure for your business in the future because you do not have to backtrack and lay the groundwork for these laws and requirements.

Other elements that your website needs to include is a landing page where your marketing ads are going to send your potential customers, as well as autoresponders to make sure your customers receive attention even when you are not online.

Finally, your website needs to have a payment processor. There are multiple platforms out there that can help you to process payments, while providing a level of security for both your company and your customers. With that in mind, let's talk about how you are going to create your product and what type of delivery system you are going to use.

Building a Product

One of the realities of producing a product is that you have to manage the logistics. Say you have come up with a product that will assist in cleaning a hard-to-reach area of the home, such as a high fan. You have your target audience and feel confident that your niche market can be expanded over time. Now you need to determine how your product is going to be produced, and then how orders will be processed.

Online businesses can offer you a variety of different options to address both these issues. You could connect with a manufacturer who produces your product and ships it when orders come in. Other manufacturers might produce the product and then ship it to a third-party fulfilment center, which then ships the orders.

You might be wondering if there are any limits to what you can sell online. The truth is that almost anything is up for grabs but determining the logistics and whether the profit margins make it viable can narrow down the field considerably.

Physical products can be anything, including homes, cars, and sports equipment. Using digital elements, such as virtual home tours, you can allow people to inspect the home, car, or sports equipment without ever leaving your home. Understand that there are a variety of items that can be sold online, and you might even be able to use a specific platform to grow your business. Some of these sites are eBay or Amazon. In that way, you do not have to create a platform from scratch, plus you get access to a larger audience than your original target audience.

Another option to consider is whether you want to offer a physical product at all. Digital products can offer several benefits that might make you want to go in that direction. For instance, a digital product can be delivered almost instantly or made available through a download. Codes and secure links can be provided, thus protecting your data while still delivering a quality product to your customers.

Digital products can also be stored cheaper and require less in terms of fulfilment and shipping costs. Your initial costs to develop the product will lessen, and the profits will increase, simply because digital products require less in terms of production and delivery.

Now that being said, you might be jumping on board the digital product train. However, you need to understand that digital products are constantly needing updates, fresh content, and more. While that might be handled by a freelance or staff computer specialist, the truth is that your digital products are not as simple as putting them in place and then leaving them to fend for themselves.

Updates to keep them relevant are a critical part of what you do. It will not necessarily be a "set it and forget it" type of business. Still, digital products and services are typically less of a capital investment than traditional physical products. If you are considering moving into a digital sphere for your product offerings, here are a few ideas to consider:

- **Online Services** – There are a variety of services that naturally lend themselves to memberships. There are special sites offering unique content related to animal training, how-to classes, and more. Physical trainers have even created online exercise classes and offered memberships to their content.

- **Social/Community Sites** – Along the same lines, these sites can offer specific information or products to your target audience while building a community that other people want to join.

- **Selling Leads** – Often, this business means building an audience and then connecting that audience with companies that provide specific services. Think insurance or other businesses that rely on leads.

- **Cost Per Action (CPA)** – Social media has produced influencers with an audience that they can offer special codes and discounts to products. Perhaps you have already built an audience or have a connection to one. Look for products that would fit with your audience and see if they have any lead affiliate options. By sharing your link, anyone who clicks through your link and makes a purchase will mean that you receive a commission based on their action.

Other digital products involve selling eBooks, CDs and DVDs, or digital packages of information, such as training or webinars. All of these can allow people to purchase items that can help them improve their skills or gain additional knowledge.

The truth is that the sky is the limit for the types of things that you can sell online, but it is important to know your audience and make sure that your offerings have a market willing to purchase them. Perhaps you already have an idea or a product, but even with your target audience in mind, you are not sure if it will be viable. With that in mind, let's move to another way to determine if your niche will work and whether there is demand. It starts with understanding some of the key aspects of online marketing, including keywords.

CHAPTER 7

Keyword Research 101

Up to this point, you have been focused on learning about your target audience, figuring out the product you want to sell, and creating a platform to sell it on. Still, when it comes to marketing online, there is one critical factor that is going to get your products and services noticed. What is it? You guessed it: keywords, and search engine optimization (SEO).

Why are keywords and SEO so important? Together, they create a system that allows search engines to direct users to your site when they are searching for information that matches your products and services.

Essentially, keywords are the search terms most frequently used by individuals when looking for different products and services or other information online. Search engines scan millions of websites daily to catalogue keywords and search terms. When someone searches for a specific phrase or keyword, then the search engines pop up the websites that have those words included.

The truth is that search engines are discovering, understanding, and organizing the internet so that when people ask questions, they get the most relevant answers. How do they manage all of that, especially with the millions of websites available and the endless amount of content?

It begins with three primary functions:

- **Crawl** – Search engines are checking for content by looking over the code and content of each URL that they encounter. Robots are sent out to find new and updated content. All the content they examine is found through links, known as URLs. The links on a blog, for instance, lead the robots to new content or even refreshed content. All those URLs will end up being indexed and retrieved if they match a search request.

- **Index** – Once they gather information in the crawling process, it has to be put into a system that organizes it, which is the index. If your website has made it to the point of being indexed, then the likelihood of your website showing up in a list of possible answers to a question increases.

- **Rank** – Each piece of content is not just randomly indexed. They are ranked based on how likely they are to give the best answer to the question being posed. That means, when you get a response back to a search on your favorite search engine, those results have already been ranked, with the most relevant answers to your question at the top.

Now let's stop for a minute and think about your last search on either Bing, Google, or any other search engine. Did you go to the second page, or did you end up clicking on a link right there on that first page? Likely, you clicked on something on that first page. That is because you assumed that the higher a website ranked on the list, the more likely it was to answer your question or provide the information that you needed.

If you are building a business, you must make sure that all of your content and pages are accessible to those search engine crawlers and allow them to index it. Otherwise, you might as well have made your page invisible. How can you determine if your pages are being indexed?

One method is to check your indexed pages on site:yourdomain.com, which is an advanced search operator. If you go to Google and type that address into the search bar, then you will be able to see what has been indexed.

While the number of results might vary, the truth is that this will give you a clear idea of what pages are being indexed and how they are showing up in search results. There are also index coverage reports available in Google Search Console. Creating an account on this console can also allow you to submit a site map of your website, thus being able to see how many of your pages have actually been indexed.

That being said, there are a few reasons why you might not be showing up in the index or search results:

- Brand new site that hasn't been crawled by a search engine

- No links to your site from any external websites

- Your navigation is challenging for a robot to crawl

- You have crawler directives in your code that are blocking search engines

- Google has penalized you for spam tactics

There is a way to tell the robots what to crawl, in order to make sure that your most important pages are indexed. There also might be pages that you do not want to become part of the index, such as old URLs, duplicate URLs, special promo pages, and test pages, to name a few. Using a method called robots.txt, you can code in specific directives to make sure that any search engine robot crawls and indexes the pages that you want to show up in searches.

Finally, it is important to know that search engines have a crawl budget, meaning they are only going to crawl so many of your URLs before it moves on to another site. Using the robot.txt file can help you maximize that budget by getting the robots focused on what is essential in your site and keeping them from wasting time on the content that is not critical.

Clearly, there is a lot that goes into making sure the robots are crawling your pages and indexing them so that your target audience can find you. As you set up your website, keeping in mind how search engines work is critical.

If you have content hidden behind login forms, then a robot is not going to be able to crawl beyond your homepage. Robots cannot use surveys, and they are not going to be logging in. Another point to keep in mind is that once a robot finds your site, they need to be able to navigate it through the internal links within your site.

Essentially, if you are starting an online business, your site needs to be structured to create a path that the robot can easily follow throughout the webpage. The fact is that you can make a mistake in navigation because you set up the desktop navigation one way, and the mobile navigation has different results. Today, everyone is shopping and searching from their phones, so mobile navigation needs to be done well so that it is crawled and indexed properly by the search engines.

All of these issues can be avoided if you create a sitemap, because it can help you to make sure that all your important URLs are listed and serve as a guide for the search engine crawlers. There are other key points that could be negatively impacting the crawlers, including errors that stop the robots from accessing your content.

In the end, as you set up your website, creating a site that is crawler friendly is key. There are a variety of tags and other coding information that should be used to help in the indexing and crawling process. However, more is needed than just getting indexed.

Every search engine has different algorithms that they use as a formula to retrieve and order the data collected from the webpages. Over the years, those algorithms have been changed to focus on improving the overall quality of their search results.

If your website suffers after an algorithm is updated, then you may need to adjust your website by reviewing content and updating it where necessary. The goal is to make sure that your content reflects the needs of the users and what they are asking for.

With all this in mind, let's focus on what is often seen as a critical part of building content, and that is the SEO.

SEO – What Is It?

To put it simply, the SEO (search engine optimization) is the process of growing both the quantity and quality of the traffic to your website by increasing your website's visibility. SEO comes into play when you are talking about building your organic search results. These are the results you get when you do not pay to have your website boosted. There are a variety of searches that come into play for SEO, including images, videos, news, industry-specific, and more.

Content is what SEO is built on, because without it, there is nothing to be consumed by the people searching for information. I can tell you that content is anything on your site, from videos, blogs, images, and descriptive text. Performing a search can result in thousands of potential answers. The better your content matches the request from the search engine, the more greatly it will increase the rank of your page on that particular search.

While some online marketing plans focus on specific keywords or content lengths, the truth is that user satisfaction is what search engines want. The truth is that search engines want to give answers that keep users coming back to them. Each of them gives guidelines, but the truth is that there is no firm list of benchmarks to meet in order to improve your rank. Creating quality content and having people link to that content are key to moving your website up the ranks.

Crosslinking within your website can be used to increase its overall visibility. One way that you can do this crosslinking is through the creation of content that includes both keywords and links back to your website. If you have older content on your website, it might no longer be effective. Therefore, it is important to keep updating your content so that the robots can crawl it frequently and get your site into more searches.

Links play a big part in SEO. Think about it like referrals or word of mouth. If you have other websites linking to yours, it gives your site more credibility and also makes it appear as an authority. If you have links from less credible sources, then it can get you flagged as spam or simply not a good authority. If you are constantly referring to yourself, then all those links can appear to be biased.

Search engines have specific programs that estimate the importance of a webpage based on who is linking to them, based on the quality and quantity of those links.

Another aspect of SEO is considering how search engines work, how their algorithms play a part in the process, what keywords are actually being searched for, and which search engines are preferred by your target audience. For instance, your target audience might prefer to use another search engine besides Google, so you might be focused on how that search engine ranks.

But SEO is a part of so many aspects of your internet marketing strategy. The better your use of keywords and SEO into your website and content, the more it will help get your website ranked higher in the search results.

Now, if your business has a physical location, you might focus on local search engine optimization to make sure your business pops up on local searches. However, if your business is solely online, then your SEO strategy is likely going to focus on large-scale searches that can come from around the world.

Here is where it can get tricky. Search engines are on the lookout for sites that try to game the system by stuffing keywords or creating what is essentially spam content. That tends to get your site banned from search engine results, which can be bad for the overall growth of your business.

The best way to manage your SEO is to write content that is relevant to your target audience and then make sure that the robots can crawl it effectively. Now let's talk about another aspect of SEO, which is how engaging your content is.

Engagement metrics reflect the data collected to see how searchers are interacting with your website. Here are what falls into those metrics:

- **Clicks** – The number of visits based on search.

- **Amount of Time Spent on Your Website** – How much time they spend on your site before they click off. The longer they stay, the better it is for the ranking of your site.

- **Bounce Rate** – The percentage of website sessions where the user only viewed one page.

- **Pogo-Sticking** – If a user clicks onto your page as part of the organic result, but then they quickly return to the search results to choose another website to visit.

The truth is that engagement metrics and SEO have a symbiotic relationship. Can you definitively say that engagement metrics move you up in the ranks, or is the engagement better because you are higher up in the search engine ranks? The truth is that many search engines choose not to share exactly how they determine their rankings, but engagement does end up playing a part.

Think about your content in terms of where it will be seen. If you are not creating pages that are easy to see and use in a mobile setting, you could be impacting how long individuals stay on your page, which can influence your ranking. To be clear, you want to have content that engages your target audience in a way that makes them not only stay longer but also want to come back.

The search landscape continues to evolve, and if your business is solely online, then you need to recognize that search engines will play a part in the process of building a connection to your target audience.

At the same time, it is important to be clear that standard organic search results might not get your website seen by as many people as other paid options meant to get you further up the list. Some of these paid options are going to be discussed in the next few chapters.

But first, let's dive into quick lead generation and how you can get your business jumpstarted to really thrive.

CHAPTER 8

Quick Traffic Generation Tactics

Online businesses flourish when they have traffic. Visitors to your website are like customers coming into a physical store. Once they are in the doors, you have a greater likelihood that they are going to buy something versus if they had not come into your store at all. The same is true of your website. If you do not have people clicking on your links and exploring your website, then you are not going to make the sales to help your business become profitable and grow.

While you might think that all you need is a few ads on social media, the truth is that there are a variety of ways to build your audience and get people to visit your website, beyond paying for ads.

Throughout this chapter, I want to focus on a few quick traffic generation tactics. While this is not an all-encompassing list, it can give you a few key areas to focus your attention to drive traffic to your website, thus growing your business by increasing your opportunities to interact with your target audience.

Content Marketing

As we discussed in the last chapter, your content can be a great way to drive traffic, because search engines are crawling your content and ranking you accordingly. However, content does have to not just be stuffed with keywords but needs to provide a benefit to your target audience, thus engaging with them and getting them willing to click and explore your website further. Here are some of the ways that you can determine if you are creating quality content for your website and social media platforms.

Write Useful Content That Answers a Question

If you consistently run across people asking variations of the same question but not finding quality answers online, then consider writing content to better answer that question. Doing so will allow search engines to send them to your site when they have someone ask that question. Think about your products and services.

What questions could your target audience have about your industry or what you offer? Could you create a blog or content that gives an answer or shares knowledge that would empower your target audience?

However, before you start building content, make sure you avoid stuffing it with keywords in an attempt to get it to register higher on the search engine rankings. High quality content might not have multiple keywords, but it will provide a valuable resource to your audience.

We have all run across an article that is written with so many keywords that the value of its content is lost. In fact, it ends up feeling as if it was written solely as clickbait. That type of content is not going to help you generate traffic or keep people coming back to your website.

Also, consider using your FAQs as a base, and expanding on them to build other types of content that matches up with your products and services. When you are writing your article, follow the best SEO practices out there, and make sure that you answer the question thoroughly. Pick content topics that are relevant now but will still have some value in the future for your target audience.

For instance, you might create a video that explains how your product works, or about its benefits, and then add that to your website as a part of a continuing series. That type of content leads me to another form of content that you can create beyond topical content reflecting the current times.

Create Evergreen Content

When it comes to content, there are certain topics that can end up being outdated or no longer relevant to the national discussion. Some content may become irrelevant as times change. Evergreen content is not likely to become outdated as some news items might. Some of these items could be:

- How-to tutorials

- Reference guides

- Product reviews

You can use this content to educate your customers and target audience. This type of content can also help to build up your authority and attract more links from other bloggers or websites, making it more likely that your site will rank higher. Plus, it stays relevant for longer periods of time. Technical questions, for instance, can be a great way to build evergreen content. Even if you need to update it from time to time, the overall content can stay consistent and provide a resource for your target audience.

Create Long-Form Content

While there are continual debates about how long content should be to get noticed by search engines, the truth is that the best content is the kind that fully addresses a topic or answers a question. Clearly, the topic will dictate length, but remember that it can be hard to cover a topic completely in just a few sentences or paragraphs. Here are a few reasons why you should consider longer content:

- Generally, it ranks better because longer content is seen as more likely to answer the questions being asked of the search engine.

- Longer content tends to be shared more often on social media.

- When content is longer, it tends to be more topically relevant, which is appealing to search engines.

- Readers can be converted into customers, which is a great way to get your target audience engaging with you and your business.

Clearly, you can build a higher level of buzz about your business and connect with your target audience through longer content forms.

If you are struggling to come up with topics for your content, then explore groups and discussion boards where your target audience is. See what they are discussing, and if you can address those topics in a meaningful way, then it would be a good way to build your content. It is also a great way to determine the keywords that will help you to create content that will show up in various searches.

Create a List Post

What is a list post? These are posts that often have titles including a number. Think of all the posts that you have seen that start with "5 reasons" or "20 top destinations," and you get the idea. Those collections or list posts tend to draw an audience, simply because they tend to draw the eye of your potential readers.

While they can bring in traffic, these types of posts are not necessarily the right type of content to convert clicks into customers. Therefore, if your content is a list type blog or video, then you still want to make sure the content is quality and is beneficial to your target audience. When you focus on what benefits your target audience, then there is a need to plan out your content, as well as the timing for publishing it.

Plan Out Content

With the continued growth of social media, platforms have been created that allow you to publish content on a schedule. That means you can write multiple articles or have video content and schedule it to pop up on your social media at intervals throughout the month. These platforms can also help you to determine the best times to schedule content, based on when your target audience is most likely to be online. Doing so increases the likelihood that your content will be seen and potentially acted upon.

For many business owners, it can be hard to keep up with regular posts on social media platforms, simply because there are so many other things that require their attention. Perhaps that has happened to you! If you want to stay relevant to your target audience, consistency is key. Your target audience will see you as a resource and a reliable source of information because you are active.

It might be tempting to post a lot of content all at once and then leave it for a while, but time and again, building a relationship with your target audience involves a steady publishing schedule.

However, if current events bring up a topic that is related to or impacts your industry, then do not be afraid to address it in your content. Shift your publishing schedule to get that relevant content out there for your audience.

If you are unclear what type of content you want to publish and when, then consider using a content calendar, which provides you a place to store ideas, plan out your content strategy, and then put things in order prior to placing them on your publishing platform. Your content calendar can also be a great place to list the content you already have created, so you can put it to use on other social media platforms.

Reuse and Repurpose

Finally, I want to focus on how you use the content you already have. Think about it this way. Creating fresh new content for every social media platform is hard work. Your target audience might primarily use Facebook, for instance, but you might also be trying to reach out to other potential market segments through other social media platforms.

Instead of trying to create fresh content for that new platform, check out the content you already have, and see if it can be repackaged or reformatted to fit. Doing so can take the pressure off constantly having to create new content. Something to note: If you are reusing content, make sure that it fits the platform. You may also need to refresh it slightly, either by editing, adding new material, or inviting comments from your target audience.

If you see that a blog of yours was particularly popular with your audience, then repackage it as a podcast, video, or e-book. Doing so allows for a fresh take on what you already know is a popular topic, but it can also be a great way to drive traffic to your site.

Republishing this content or even reposting updated blogs will increase your visibility on search engines. Your website will end up popping up higher on the search results, especially as the robots locate your newer content and find it to be more valuable to users.

Now that you have built a content library, focusing on either your products, your services, or that which imparts knowledge about industry, you need to find a way to get that content out there.

Connecting with Your Target Audience

When you are first starting out in business, building an audience for your content and then driving that audience to your business can be challenging. Too often, you put out the content, but it does not get many views initially. It can be frustrating because you are competing against so many pieces of content, plus you are dealing with the fact that your audience is smaller initially.

One of the best ways to get noticed and grow your audience is by connecting with influencers. Remember that search engines are going to rank your content higher if it is linked to by other sites. If you invite guest bloggers from within your industry, who already have a sizable audience, then they are going to connect back to that blog and increase the traffic to your site.

Connecting with other bloggers and getting them to interview you is another way to draw traffic and interest to your site. By creating connections and building a network with influencers within your niche market, your site will start to rank higher but also grow its audience. An additional option is to partner with another blogger or business that has a common interest or complimentary products.

A word of caution when it comes to posting guest blogs or content on other websites: You may find that even though it has backlinks to your website, that content is also driving traffic to other websites. You may end up losing your audience because they are distracted by other content or businesses.

By building up market-friendly content themes, and using content partners and guest bloggers, you can build up your audience. Once that audience is created, you can build in additional calls to action on your website to get them into your sales funnel.

Another method to generate leads returns you to social media. That platform can allow you to increase your ranking in search engines, but also expose you to a larger audience. Think of it this way. You put together an interesting video piece showcasing your latest product. Then you share it on social media. Three people share it, and each of those individuals has three more people share it. The sharing continues, and your content ends up having a larger reach than you anticipated.

The more frequently you post content, the more likely your content will be shared. In fact, some search engines prioritize websites with higher social media shares. With quality content, you can increase the likelihood of getting a cut of those social media shares and building your audience.

Are You Engaging with Your Audience?

It does not mean just creating content, putting it out on various platforms, and then never revisiting it. Time and again on social media, content creators put out the content but never check the comments and respond to any of them. They might even ask a question, yet they do not engage with the audience when they comment. Eventually, those individuals stop engaging and sharing your content.

I encourage you to take the time to read through the comments. Whenever possible, write a response or add more to the discussion. The audience will stay engaged and start sharing the content, helping your audience to grow.

There are plenty of ways to build traffic up and generate leads in an organic way that allows you to build an audience and a customer base for your business. Now that you have an idea of type of content that builds traffic, let's get into the different platforms where digital marketing can be the key to move your business to the next level.

CHAPTER 9

Marketing Options— Social Media and Mobile

Having an online business means taking a different marketing tack than you would for a bricks and mortar location. After all, you are not limited to a specific geographical location, so your marketing needs to be appealing to members of your target audience from around the globe.

Today's social media and internet platforms provide a variety of tools that allow you to make specific marketing choices. With that in mind, let's discuss the different types of advertising and marketing options available online and how they can be used to grow your business.

Facebook Marketing

The goal of Facebook Marketing is to get your page and ads in front of the people who most likely fit your target audience in both organic and paid-for ways. To get started, create a Facebook page for your business. It gives you a platform to start reaching out to individuals, inviting them to like your page and learn about your business. Include a detailed "about" page, where you talk about what you do, why your customers should choose to do business with you, and any other unique details that make your business stand out.

Where a Facebook profile requires you to have mutual friend relationships for your posts to be seen in people's newsfeeds, a page can be liked by anyone who might be interested in your products or services. That gives you the ability to connect with people that might not even typically fall into your target audience.

Your page can be customized to show off the human side of your business and develop your brand identity more fully. For instance, you might put up a funny video about a challenge in your industry that your target audience can

Book.Simply123ToSuccess.com

identify with, and then put up links to your business and how you address that challenge.

Someone selling shoes might put up a funny video with dogs and tiny shoes, and then follow up with a quality article about how to measure your shoe size accurately, or even the type of inserts there are to address different foot issues. Note that a mix of humor and education can make your page stand out to your target audience.

Contests can also be a way to draw your target audience to explore your products and services, as well as being a great way to build your lists and get feedback on your target audience. Choose a product or service that you want to highlight, and then use it as part of the contest to draw the attention of your target audience.

One of the things about your page's posts that is critical to growing clicks to your webpage, is making sure that it links back to your products, services, and content. The challenge with these pages is that it can be difficult to build a fan base and stand out from all the other pages out there.

To help with that process, consider the content you are posting. Make sure the content is informative and useful. Do not be quick to post just to check that off on a box, thus making you feel that you did something. When you are focused on posting just to post, your followers are going to get frustrated because your content is clogging their newsfeed with what they perceive as junk.

What defines quality content? Beneficial things to post include links to helpful articles regarding your industry, product announcements, codes for sales or discounts, and even links to blog, vlogs, or other content living on your webpage. The average Facebook user is dealing with ads constantly; to

Marketing Options—Social Media and Mobile

stand out, you need succinct copy, striking visuals, and video content that grabs their attention. Just make sure you provide content that gives your audience something they did not have before, and they will stay connected with your business.

When it comes to attracting a larger fan base, you can use Facebook ads. Their targeted ad platform allows you to use content made for your website, or other platforms could be used here.

Plus, you can aim those ads to specific geographical areas, education levels, ages, or even specific devices that are being used to browse through Facebook newsfeeds. The best part is that people can not only look at your ad and click through to your webpage, but they can also close the ad and then go to your Facebook page and like it to receive your posts in their newsfeed.

The challenge with these ads is that it can get expensive, depending on how large a reach you want to have with your target audience. To get the most out of these purchased ads, it is important to set a budget but also to collect data about what ads seem to be working well and which ones are not connecting with your target audience.

The other benefit of these Facebook targeted ads is that you can customize ads to meet the needs of different various demographic groups, thus strengthening their connections to your brand. Better-targeted ads give you better results and deeper connections with your target audience.

Owning an online business means collecting and analysing data to better understand how your target audience behaves online and where you can best build relationships with them. However, the beauty of social media is that there are multiple ways to connect with each other.

Facebook groups is one such way. Essentially, you are creating a discussion forum where members of your target audience can discuss things related to your products and services. You can also use it as a platform to reach out to perspective customers. A word of caution if you decide to set up a Facebook group: You want to be engaged in the group. Questions are going to come up, and engagement is what you need to build relationships. If they do not see you engaging, eventually they will stop, and you will find that what you hoped to gain from the group is lost.

Use the group to ask open-ended questions and get a feel about what your audience likes, or even learn about products or services that they would like to see. When they see you interacting with them, then they feel that your business values their opinions and feedback, which can help you rise in their newsfeed and increase your overall engagement with your target audience.

The truth is that Facebook has a large audience and the potential to give your business a quality ROI, but it will not be effective if you do not use it well. To get the maximum amount of benefit, build your ads around the goals and objectives of your business. Are you trying to build awareness, consideration, or conversion? Your ads need to reflect those goals. If your content is unclear, then you are unlikely to get your audience to do what you want.

Track how the ads are doing and be open to adjusting ads to make them work better based on the numbers. After all, you can see whether an ad is getting a good response or a poor one. If it is a poor one, then consider pulling that ad and altering the content. Comments on ads can also be a great source of feedback to tell you what is working and what is not. That feedback is key to adjusting your content.

Marketing Options—Social Media and Mobile

The options on Facebook for marketing are endless, from simple lead generation to conversion. Dabbling is not going to be the best use of your resources. Instead, use that platform as a staple of your marketing plan to create growth.

However, Facebook is not the only platform out there. Google has a variety of options that can also help you to grow the reach of your business. Let's dive into some of the options available on the largest search platform on the internet.

Google Advertising and Shopping

Both Google Advertising and Shopping provide excellent ways to draw traffic and conversions to your website. Google Shopping, which was formerly known as Google Product Listing Ads (or PLAs), gives website owners the ability to set their desired costs per click in order to have their product ad at the top of Google's search results. You can include product pictures. This option also gives you the ability to moderate your bids based on individual products, product groupings, and your daily budget. What makes this a nice option is that you do not need to set up text or bid on any keywords. If you are creating an online business focused on ecommerce, then this might be a viable option, especially if you have a product feed or carry a large volume of different products.

Google Ads, on the other hand, is an option that allows website owners to bid on specific keywords, thus putting their ads at the top of searches where those keywords are used. However, while this option can also be used for ecommerce, it is geared toward sites with a smaller volume of products.

There are also more controls available for you regarding your advertisement messaging, branding, and sales information.

The question you might be asking yourself is what will work best for your business. The answer depends on your business and what you are offering. If you have a large number of products, then you could set up a landing page for each one, using Google Shopping. This option's pay per click (PPC) often results in a higher click-through rate. Unfortunately for your budget, more clicks can also mean a higher cost for your business.

Still, when you run the numbers, that higher click-through rate can be more appealing, simply because you make back the money for all those clicks with more orders. After all, once they click through to your website, the chances of them staying and making a purchase have increased.

If you are creating a Google Shopping marketing campaign, then here are three best practices to keep in mind. First, maintain your product fee and product data quality. If your data does not match your website, then Google will not show your ads. Second, optimize your products and create unique product categories. Also, make sure that all your product shots are unique, high-quality images and not stock ones. Third, you want to optimize your products and services for big events, to make sure you are ready for any increase in traffic.

The last thing that you want to happen during a sale or increase in click-throughs is for your website to load slowly or even crash. There are clearly other aspects of Google ads, which can benefit your online business, but for now, it is important to know that you are putting your business in a position to be seen at a point when people are actively looking for your type of products and services.

Marketing Options—Social Media and Mobile

Social Media Platforms

While I did spend some time focusing on Facebook, due to its prominence in the social media marketing space, the truth is that there are several different social media platforms where you can reach out to your target audience. For instance, you might be offering training and leadership materials as part of your product offerings. That type of offering might find a more receptive audience on LinkedIn or other professional platforms, instead of on a social media platform geared toward individuals connecting with each other for personal reasons.

Each platform has its own type of ad space, and many of them follow basic patterns of paying for your ad to be elevated or a PPC system. Either way, your marketing campaign on these platforms needs to be based on your target audience.

For instance, if your target audience is not known to spend time on Instagram, then you probably do not want to spend time and energy putting out content and building ads for that space. There are also a variety of nuances that can impact how you invest in social media marketing.

Each platform has its unique attributes as well. For instance, Twitter is a great social app for getting feedback from customers. Other platforms offer visually compelling options, like Instagram. The point is to maximize the benefits of the platforms you choose to use with your business.

Here are a few things to keep in mind:

1. If you are marketing directly to a business, then LinkedIn is likely the better platform.

103

2. If you are marketing to consumers, then using Facebook and Instagram can help you to grow your visibility.

3. YouTube is a channel that every business can use to interact; plus, it is Google-friendly.

Remember, the demographics of your target audience will also be an important guide. Once you dive into them, then you can narrow down your platform to the one that is most beneficial. It is also about putting energy into a platform where your target customer is spending their time and not wasting your resources.

When you first start out, it can be easy to overwhelm yourself by trying to market across multiple platforms. I would caution against that because it would mean spreading yourself thin. Put some time and effort into the platform you choose, to create quality ad content and engagement with your target audience. When you are trying to do too much on too many platforms, then you risk the quality of your marketing.

Where are your competitors? If you are struggling to find the right platform, look for where your competitors are hanging out. That might give you a few ideas about where you might want to spend your time. Still, do not be quick to follow the crowd. After all, they might be plunking resources in social media platforms without a quality marketing strategy. Therefore, you should first focus on your demographics and then check out your competitors to avoid potentially making a mistake that leaves you with a limited ROI.

Finally, all this marketing on social media is not going to be worth anything if you do not make sure to invest in your website. Building a quality website is critical because it is where your customers are coming to learn about and

Marketing Options—Social Media and Mobile

purchase your products. Make sure that it is easy to navigate, that your links are up to date, and that it loads quickly.

There are many platforms meant to help you build a website, but the truth is that just because you can DIY, it does not mean that you should. After all, you want your business cards, website, and any marketing to be consistent and reflect your brand well. Plus, your website is going to be seen everywhere, so when people land there, you want them to quickly engage with what you have available.

Another key point to stress here is that you need to create a social media strategy that will be maintainable. After all, you do not want to spread yourself too thin, but the truth is that a consistent strategy is more critical to being successful on any social media platform. Doing so will help you connect and engage with the customers.

Mobile Marketing

First, let's define what mobile marketing is. Essentially, it is the art of marketing your business in a way that is appealing to mobile device users. When you do it right, then you are providing your business an additional way to connect with customers, or potential customers, by giving them personalized and location sensitive information. Now they can get the information they need, exactly when they need it.

Mobile marketing has become even more prevalent in the last few years. Google has even put together apps that allow for business ads to pop up when an individual passes by the business. Smartphone apps are also geared to help people find what they are looking for based on their location.

Book.Simply123ToSuccess.com

Having a mobile marketing strategy is key, especially as people continue to gravitate to their devices. For instance, 80% of mobile device time is spent on apps, and more than 70% of web pages are browsed on tablets versus smartphones. Conversions are growing on mobile devices, meaning that people are making purchasing decisions right on their mobile devices, including smartphones and tablets.

Clearly, that means you need to be making sure that your business is mobile friendly. Here are a few strategies to consider as you implement mobile marketing.

App-based marketing is mobile ads done through mobile apps. You do not have to create an app to enjoy the benefits of this marketing strategy. Services, such as Google AdMob, can help you to create mobile ads that appear on third-party mobile apps, including gaming ones that capture many people's attention.

Facebook, of course, has a platform to allow for the integration of your ads into their newsfeeds on a mobile device, so you can still be connecting with your customers even if they are scrolling on their phones.

Another option is QR codes, which can be scanned by users, allowing them to get right to the landing page on your website where a specific product or service is featured. Another option is using text messages, allowing people to opt in as part of your list, and receive special offers via text.

One of the cautions I want to share is that content and ads need to be optimized for mobile devices. Your content may lose its ability to connect with your audience if they cannot see it well or have to continually scroll in order to read everything you have to say. Spend the time to make sure your

Marketing Options—Social Media and Mobile

content will look right on each platform before putting it out; otherwise, your audience could end up getting turned off or frustrated.

As you can see, there are a variety of online options to allow your business to connect with your target audience. They can click through your content, links, ads, and mobile marketing to reach your website. The possibilities are truly endless for marketing and growing your relationships with your target audience.

Throughout these chapters, I have covered a lot of information about setting up an online business, and the benefits of doing so. There has also been a detailed discussion of the right steps to take to create a foundation for growth. When you do the right things at the start, then your business has the ability to become a long-term income stream.

Now that we have focused on building an online business and marketing it effectively, let's talk about the importance of having the right mindset and how it contributes to building your success.

CHAPTER 10

Have the Right Mindset

Building a business, whether sticks and bricks or online, requires a focused mindset and a determination to continue moving forward despite the challenges and setbacks. There is rarely a business that is an instant success. Behind every success is a leader determined to look past the failures to find the solutions their business needs to take it to the next level.

Online businesses also require leaders to see failure as a way to learn and refine their systems, processes, and marketing strategies. As online advertising and marketing continue to shift with technology, marketers can refine their messages even further to target various customers and audiences. There is another advantage to online businesses. They often allow for shifting in the direction of your business based on what is happening right now.

Entrepreneurs thrive on being able to address the current climate, moving quickly to shift away from what is not working, and shifting toward what is working. Think about marketing from that entrepreneurial perspective. Old marketing strategies involved putting out ads on television, radio, print mediums, and billboards. Then it would take several months to collect the data to determine what worked and what did not. The campaign would be adjusted, and that process would start all over again.

Today's marketing strategies incorporate online options, and that means data is being collected instantly. Changes can be made in a matter of days or even hours, depending on the feedback and data collected. The old way of doing things means your business could end up looking like it was standing still, simply because those older marketing strategies did not allow a business to be nimble enough.

As you open your online business, I want you to embrace the entrepreneurial mindset. Be aware of what is going on in your industry and with your target audience. Open your mind to making changes and keeping your business nimble, allowing you to shift when a new opportunity for your products arises, as well as giving yourself permission to let go of products or services that are no longer serving your business.

Another aspect of being nimble means thinking outside of the box. You can do the research and target a specific audience, only to find that another demographic is also interested in your products. They do not fit your ideal customer, but they are interested and willing to buy. Being nimble means that you embrace these customers, even if it means shifting your messaging slightly to reach them.

Throughout the journey of building your online business, there are going to be times when you take a misstep. Your audience might not respond to content, or it might take longer to build your core audience through social media than you anticipated. As a leader, you have to choose the mindset that you will use to lead your team and guide your business throughout all its stages.

What Are the Two Mindsets Driving Leadership?

There are two different mindsets. The first is a fixed mindset, which tends to demonstrate itself in a variety of ways. A fixed mindset sees failure as a judgment about their leadership, so they view themselves as a failure. It becomes a part of how a business leader views themselves and their business. They are unlikely to take risks; or worse, they tend to just follow the crowd without a clear definition of their business's direction.

A fixed mindset will keep a leader from trying new things, afraid of upsetting the status quo. It depends on external validation for success or

Have the Right Mindset

failure. That often means a business is not nimble enough to create change when needed. The survival of the business depends on others, and there is a sense of helplessness, as if you do not have the control and ability to lead your business where it needs to go.

On the other hand, a growth mindset is a belief that your abilities as a leader can be learned and developed, and that you can create meaningful change through hard work and perseverance. Having a growth mindset means that you focus on what you can learn and how you can adjust from these experiences to shift your marketing and the direction of your business.

How you think determines how you feel and how you behave, and your behavior determines the outcome. Essentially, if you think you will succeed, then you are right. If you think that you will fail, then you are right. These principles are true, but even more so when it comes to leading your online business.

In running your business, you have the ability to try, fail, and learn from those experiences. As a leader, you can move at a different pace than you have ever moved before and can overcome obstacles. Start thinking about how you can make things happen, rather than what cannot be changed.

A growth mindset in a leader means embracing different viewpoints, seizing on previously unseen opportunities, and tapping into the variety of skills available on their team. How can you foster a growth mindset in yourself and your team?

First, be open-minded and inclusive of the unique needs and perspectives of others, particularly your target audience. It is more than focusing just on sales and revenue; it is focusing on your assets of your team and how they can be used to address the needs of your consumers and employees.

Book.Simply123ToSuccess.com

Another important aspect of a growth mindset is recognizing that you cannot always plan for every contingency. Many businesses, particularly ones based online, operate in environments where ambiguity and uncertainty are part of the reality of doing business. However, that ambiguity and uncertainty can also expose a variety of opportunities. Embrace it and use those opportunities to create momentum and sustain it.

Part of a growth mindset is having situational awareness and the ability to see around, beneath, and beyond what you seek. It is essentially the difference between circular and linear vision.

As a leader, you need to avoid a linear perspective that has you trying to be in control at all times. Instead, a growth mindset allows you to activate those around you to use their influence to achieve even more. It is about utilizing the resources and assets of the organization in ways that drive and guide growth opportunities.

Too many organizations suffer from linear perspectives, and that means they are not in a position to transform and shift as their market changes. Linear thinking and a fixed mindset mean spending millions in planning but failing to operationalize that planning effectively in their business. They fail to anticipate the unexpected and are not prepared to face the strategic implications of investments and uncertainty involved in bringing transformation to fruition.

With a growth mindset, you have a clarity about what others are expecting from you. Ultimately, it is about thinking about your business differently and taking on new, elevated levels of ownership as a leader. Be clear about the path to growth and the role that your team members are going to play in order to get your organization there.

Have the Right Mindset

Building an online business involves taking ownership, keeping your business relevant instead of letting the marketplace pass you by because you get complacent in how you deliver your products and services to your customers. Complacency makes you appear as if you do not care enough. That impression rubs off on your team and impacts the ability of your business to thrive.

Complacency in your mindset also means you might be closed off to various opportunities or new avenues to grow your business. The very nature of the online world gives your business the opportunity to shift quickly. Your success is based upon the ability of your business to adapt and change. Do not fall into the mindset that wants to set things up and then leave your business to run itself.

Throughout these chapters, I have shared key principles and ideas to build an online business and then market it effectively. However, as part of this journey, I also understand that every business will face challenges and opportunities. Your mindset is how you choose what to pursue and what to turn away from as you build your business.

Success or Failure Is a State of Mind

One of the things that I have seen in business after business is that the mindset of the leadership is key to its success or failure. Leaders with a growth mindset focus on learning, adjusting, and adapting. They do not see failure as a reason to quit.

Instead, use your marketing strategy to showcase the knowledge, capabilities, and skill sets of your business and its team. That builds executive presence, which requires self-confidence, self-trust, the ability to navigate the needs of people, and self-awareness. Your mindset defines whether you are focused on others and building relationships or limited in your ability to grow personally and professionally.

Clearly, you want to be a leader with a growth mindset because it gives you the ability to grow and elevate your business to the next level. Even the best marketing strategy cannot effectively build an online business if your mindset is closed and fixed. The opportunities will never show themselves, and your business will continue to struggle.

Leaders with a growth mindset desire to be significant because they want to take their organization to places it had never been before, and to truly evolve to the next level. See the opportunities available through online marketing as the means to build relationships with your customers and help them to see how your products and services can be the answer to their problems.

Owning a business means providing solutions for your customers and target audience. Your content and messaging are a way for you to build a connection and help them to see how your products and services meet their needs. Since you are not in front of your customers in a traditional "sticks and bricks," then your content needs to work even harder to deliver your message clearly, and thus inspire your target customers to try your products.

The world is transitioning to a wisdom-based economy, where it is about what you do with what you know. The products and services you offer should be based on what you know but also about being open to learning and working hard to grow.

Your growth mindset is evident by how you behave, how you deal with customer feedback and complaints, and most importantly, how you deal with failure. When your orders are backed up at the fulfilment center, are you

Have the Right Mindset

going to throw up your hands and just quit, or are you going to work with the fulfilment center and your customers to get things moving again?

Online businesses often rely on others for the final leg of delivery of their product to their customers. Understand how that process works and be open to making changes when one aspect of your fulfilment process is no longer working.

Be Creative and Curious

Discussing mindset means understanding how a growth mindset plays into building any type of business. However, to see the opportunities that will enable the growth your business, your mindset needs to foster your curiosity and creativity. Not every customer is going to see your products as addressing a need they have. When you are curious and creative, you can actually help your customers to see a need they did not even realize that they had.

Collaborate with your team to learn the problems of your target audience and then how your products can address those problems. It might also mean that you need to rethink how your products are used, or even develop new products or accessories to allow your current line-up to be more versatile.

Too often, a fixed mindset can crop up, where we only see our products as addressing one issue, when there are more possibilities available if you are curious enough to look for them.

That adaptability through curiosity and creativity is key to keeping your business relevant and as a leader in the marketplace. With new online businesses constantly popping up, your marketing needs to complement your business and help it to stand out. That means your content needs to reflect your curiosity and creativity.

When you are curious, then you look beyond the current climate and find the trends that speak to your business. Curiosity is about looking for those opportunities and finding the next big thing for your business. Build a platform for transformation that allows for change and growth.

Never stop trying to find ways to improve. No matter how well a product or service does, that never means it cannot get any better. Be curious about what your customers think of your products and their experiences. Find ways to interact with them, so you can envision what they expect and then meet those expectations successfully.

Online businesses have a unique way to gather that feedback, through their social media platforms and surveys, as well as answering direct questions from customers. Use those mediums to learn and grow. Do not make excuses and shut down, because that demonstrates a fixed mindset. Instead, focus on what you can adapt, learn, and change.

While it can be easy to get defensive when confronted with negative reviews or feedback, the truth is that feedback can be critical to address weaknesses within your business. My goal in working with online business owners is to help them not only set up a successful business, but to give them the mindset tools to fuel that success.

Perhaps you are on the fence about taking the step to start your online business. My hope is that with the guidelines, principles, and steps found within these chapters, you can take that next step to fulfil your dream of owning a business. Use them to not only create a marketing strategy, but

Have the Right Mindset

to find the right niche, the right product, and to set the foundation for your online business.

Fuel your passion to live your entrepreneurial dreams. I would love to hear more about your experiences and connect with you personally, please go to marketing.trueproductsnetwork.com. Let's build a marketing strategy to create and grow your online business.

ABOUT THE AUTHOR

Hello; my name is Nigel Lear, and I live in England, UK. I want to take a second to say "hello" and "welcome."

This is not the usual "welcome" you get for joining some email list. Think of it more like a firm handshake you would get before starting an adventure.

Because that is what this is: the adventure of gaining more control of your life—your time, your freedom, and your income.

With that handshake, you have my promise that I will be straight with you and not waste your time or mine—fair enough?

I should tell you a little about myself . . .

I am a professional digital marketer, business start-up and traffic strategy coach, trainer, and best-selling author of 2 books, with a sales, IT, and marketing background. I have spent 25+ years underneath dusty desks, answering support calls, and installing web servers in noisy data centers.

On route, I have worked with some of the best web designers, marketers, and businesses in the world. I would like to share some of that knowledge and experience with you.

I work in my digital marketing business (True Products Marketing), coaching and educational business (Nigellear.com), and data network Infrastructure business (True Products Network Ltd).

About the Author

I have recently started a new consultancy business, transforming and shifting paradigms to where you want to go, with a revolutionary step-by-step process endorsed by the Proctor Gallagher Institute. Email me at book@simply123tosuccess.com if you would like me to show you more.

Online marketing is a subject close to my heart, where I am helping businesses, entrepreneurs, stay-at-home moms, and committed individuals to fulfil their potential and dreams.

I have developed a unique business platform, and with this book, it will make it possible, creating an online presence with demand, without the know-how and technical skills. All you require is an idea—truly magical and unique!

Here is the incredible news: You can get anything you truly desire!

I believe that learning has no value unless you walk away with something that you actually use. I love to travel and help people of all walks of life to achieve their dreams.

I can help you to overcome obstacles and achieve great things in life and business.

The author is available for delivering keynote presentations to appropriate audiences. For rates and availability, please contact the author directly at book@simply123tosuccess.com

To order more books, please visit www.amazon.com

Finally, if you have been inspired by this book, the best thing you could ever do is pass it on and be a wonderful role model for others. This world needs more action takers, like you.

Made in the USA
Monee, IL
06 April 2021